D0875095

Reader Testimonies
Christ Our Healer: A Revelation of Mercy

Healed from Bladder Cancer
(Excerpts from the Introduction)

I am very thankful that Greg wrote this book, because it was a key instrument that God used to help me to get healed from the cancer. It is well written, easy to understand, and very helpful. . . .Although I have been through some ups and downs while battling bladder cancer, God has used the book as a great tool for strengthening my faith. . . .The cancer was so serious that the doctors wanted to do chemotherapy and radiation and also wanted to cut out my bladder, urethra, and prostate . . . [but] I said "no" to the chemo, radiation, and cutting. . . .I decided to pursue elevating my faith, and I read Greg's book over and over again.

Finally, in September of 2014, the biopsy came back from the doctor and I was as clean as a whistle—I was cancer-free!

This is the best book I ever read. Just as I did, I encourage you to read this book over and over again until the principles truly take hold of your life. What God did for me, he can also do for you, because He is a God of great mercy and compassion!

—Daniel Kelly
Programmer Analyst Level III
Gettysburg, PA

Overcame Fears and Received Hope

When someone receives a diagnosis of cancer or cancer returns, there is often fear. I had a tumor (ovarian) that grew very large, very fast. Surgery was necessary to remove it and the success rate for treatment is poor; only one in seven women respond to the chemotherapy. I decided not to do the chemo.

When I came home from the hospital, my friend Dan Kelly gave me the book *Christ Our Healer: A Revelation of Mercy* by Gregory Dixon to read. By the grace of God, Dan overcame bladder cancer with the help of this book, and he understood what I was facing. This book helped to strengthen my faith, put many fears to rest, and taught about the mercy of Christ. Even though I was weak physically, mentally, and spiritually, the book was very easy to read and understand. It gave me the hope I needed in a very dark time and ministered to me with healing scriptures. Since then, I have ordered copies of this book to give to others that are facing difficult health situations.

—Laura Starner
Banking Industry Customer Relations Professional
Mechanicsburg, PA

Impacted a Church

Words can't express what I felt when I first read the book *Christ Our Healer: A Revelation of Mercy* by Greg Dixon. It far exceeded my expectations! Greg has done a marvelous job of condensing the essentials of healing principles from the original version; making it so much more user-friendly. I am a registered nurse and I also lead the "Victory Seekers" cancer support group at my church, so I am in contact with lots of people who need healing. I know so many lives will be rescued for the kingdom. Thanks, Greg, for all you are doing to make known the healing power of Jesus! The books are still doing the job that they were designed to do, so I want to have extra copies available whenever I can.

I recall giving one of these books to a man with fresh prostate cancer and he was very greatly impacted by it. He is an educational doctor along with his wife. The book has proven to be extremely valuable in terms of aiding the healing of these desperate people and we are grateful for the help they are receiving because God has entrusted us to help these precious individuals.

I am thankful that Greg has given so much of himself and his time to enlighten the hungry people of my church—Christian Life Assembly—as far as healing in light of God's wonderful mercy. The book has opened up an avenue of faith and interest that will continue to be explored.

—Cheryl Lehmann
Registered Nurse
and C.L.A. Victory Seekers Group Leader
Camp Hill, PA

Christ our Healer

A Revelation of Mercy

Christ our Healer

A Revelation of Mercy

GREGORY A. DIXON

P.O. Box 23927
Jacksonville, Florida 32241
www.impactcommunications.net

Christ Our Healer: A Revelation of Mercy

Published in Jacksonville, Florida, by Impact Communications

Website:
www.impactcommunications.net

Mailing Address:
Impact Communications
P.O. Box 23927
Jacksonville, Florida 32241

ISBN: 978-0-9742297-6-8

This book based primarily on the life and teachings of Fred Francis Bosworth has been compiled and written by Gregory A. Dixon. Unless specifically stated to be a direct quote or general statement by Fred Francis Bosworth or another specifically stated author, all statements in this book are ascribed to Gregory A. Dixon.

Italics used in Scripture are the author's emphasis.

Unless otherwise indicated, Scripture quotations are from:

The Holy Bible, King James Version

Other Scripture quotations are from:

The Holy Bible, New King James Version (NKJV)
© 1984 by Thomas Nelson, Inc.

Printed in the United States of America

IMPG6-21-2016B00000

DEDICATION

This book is dedicated to Cheryl Lehmann because she is the one who unknowingly inspired me to write it one day when she exposed me to Bosworth's original book and also shared some of her testimony in a Christian bookstore. Cheryl has also kept me encouraged over the years and has encouraged me at times to continue spreading the message of this book when I was tempted to get off track because of the cares of this world. She is a true inspiration and a bright and shining light in a world that is in desperate need of God's mercy and grace, especially as it relates to physical healing. Over the years, I have seen her overcome many setbacks and many obstacles by the grace of God. She is a true example that in Christ there is victory over sickness and death, and I am very grateful for her contributions to this book. I truly owe the creation of this book to God and to Cheryl Lehmann.

TABLE OF CONTENTS

Appendix

FOREWORD

In spite of the enormous amount of money spent on health care in our present American culture, the amount of individuals who continually suffer or die from fatal diseases is staggering. Where is God? Does He not heal today as He did in the days of the Bible? Has Jesus fallen asleep or lost His power? Did miracles pass away with the apostles?

Being a Christian now for 30-plus years and being in full-time ministry for nearly 20 years, I've wondered this myself and have heard thousands of others ask these same questions.

These questions put me on a personal search to find answers, which led to reading over 30 books on the topic of divine healing. After beginning to read some of these books and search the Scriptures myself, I was healed of an incurable disease. I thank God for His Word and the mercy He had on me and for faithful men and women who have taken the time to bring forth the absolute truth that God still heals today.

Greg Dixon is one of these men. Inspired by the teachings of F.F. Bosworth, one of the pioneers of the divine healing message, Greg has done a fabulous job of simplifying Bosworth's masterpiece, *Christ the Healer.*

Christ the Healer was a book that influenced many of the great healing evangelists in the early- and mid-1900s. Greg has taken the timeless truths in that book and broken them down into 10 easy-to-understand principles. Furthermore, in addition to skillfully condensing and illuminating Bosworth's teachings, Greg has added even more clarity to the message of divine healing with extra Scripture references, along with many contemporary stories from credible ministers.

I have had the privilege of fellowshipping with Greg at our weekly worship service for some time now, and I am blessed by his passion for the Lord. He has a firm stance to live by the Word and to help others understand and do the same. I believe that this book will bring understanding and encourage your faith to personally experience God and His promises as it has done for me.

The key to experiencing the promises of God in our own lives is to have proper knowledge and understanding of His Word. Contrary to the popular statement "What you don't know won't hurt you," God says what you don't know could actually kill you. Hosea 4:6 says "My people are destroyed for lack of knowledge."

Will God ever heal? Will God always heal? Why do some people receive healing and others don't? Have you ever made the statement, "I know God can heal me; I'm just not sure if it's His will"?

I encourage you to look inside *Christ Our Healer: A Revelation of Mercy* by Gregory Dixon to find these answers for yourself. Take your time as you read and allow the Word of God and the principles which are communicated to get into your heart. Be honest as you read and don't let your preconceived ideas or things you have been taught block you from gaining what God desires for you. Life or death could be the difference—if not yours, then somebody else's. Jesus said, "If you continue in my word, then are you my disciples indeed; and you shall know the truth, and the truth shall make you free" (John 8:31-32).

—Danon S. Winter
Director of Charis Bible College Florida,
an extension of Andrew Wommack Ministries

INTRODUCTION

How God Healed Me of Bladder Cancer

By Daniel Kelly

Jean Reist from Journey to Wellness in Dillsburg, Pennsylvania, gave me a copy of *Christ Our Healer: A Revelation of Mercy* by Gregory Dixon back in February of 2014 while I was dealing with bladder cancer. I am very thankful that Greg wrote this book, because it was a key instrument that God used to help me to get healed from the cancer. It is well written, easy to understand, and very helpful. I have since read Bosworth's original book, *Christ the Healer*, once (my son let me have his copy that he got when he attended Rhema Bible Training College), and I have read Greg Dixon's book several times. I have also purchased several copies of *Christ Our Healer: A Revelation of Mercy* by Gregory Dixon for the purpose of giving them away to people in need. I probably also need to keep an extra book for myself before my current copy gets worn out!

Although I have been through some ups and downs while battling bladder cancer, God has used the book as a great tool for strengthening my faith. In early December of 2013 I discovered that the bladder cancer returned to my body for the third time after my urologist at Hershey Medical Center did a biopsy. At this point, I already had several surgeries.

The cancer was so serious that the doctors wanted to do chemotherapy and radiation and also wanted to cut out my bladder, urethra, and prostate. I thought this was too radical and didn't want to do it so I said "no" to the chemo, radiation, and cutting, but asked my urologist to still keep me under his care. During this ordeal, I felt the need to enlist the help of a holistic doctor to start changing my lifestyle—spirit, soul, and body.

This was around the time I went to see Jean Reist, the holistic practitioner from "Journey to Wellness" in Dillsburg, Pennsylvania, who embraces Christ as the ultimate healer. She handed me the book

Christ Our Healer: A Revelation of Mercy by Gregory Dixon and I was extremely skeptical at first. But I really looked at the book when I got home, and the book impacted my life in a much greater way than I expected.

I also read Bosworth's original book, along with reading *Healing the Sick* by T.L. Osborn. But Gregory Dixon's book was most important to me and had the greatest impact on my life. I immediately connected to him through his book, and the principles in it really encouraged me to do what the Word says. The first chapter, "Starve Doubt and Feed Faith," had a great impact on me. I was also greatly impacted by the chapter about Jesus redeeming us from our diseases when he atoned for our sins. But the biggest part of the book was the chapter titled, "A Revelation of Mercy." That's what really changed my life the most. I did not really understand God's mercy and I was very works-oriented—maybe because of my Catholic upbringing. And Gregory Dixon's chapter about God's mercy is what really breathed new life into me and made a huge difference.

This says a lot about his book, because I was no stranger to the healing message when I first read it. I was introduced to Pop Hagin's teachings over 30 years ago and have known the healing message for a long time. Another reason I was no stranger to the healing message was because my parents went to Rhema Bible Training College, founded by Kenneth Hagin.

While reading Gregory Dixon's book over and over, I also read a particular chapter in T.L. Osborn's book that inspired me to start taking communion a lot—every couple of days. While doing this, I continued to pour through Gregory Dixon's book all the more. Although the book was encouraging me to trust God for healing, I still played my part and went back to the urologist every couple of months. The doctor still recommended chemo, radiation, and cutting everything out. I said, "No. I do not want to lose my body parts." I decided to pursue elevating my faith and I read Greg's book over and over again. I saw the doctor several times and he continued to recommend the radical treatments. But I continued to refuse them while leaning on Scriptures like Hebrews 6:12 and Hebrews 10:35. I made up my mind that I would be like the determined woman in the Bible with the issue of blood.

Finally, in September of 2014, a biopsy came back from the doctor, and I was as clean as a whistle—I was cancer-free! I was first diagnosed with cancer in 2007, so I was grateful to be cancer-free after such a challenging journey.

The doctor told me, "I don't know what you are doing but just keep on doing it. You should write a book about it."

In disbelief, the doctor said, "Let's check again."

He did another biopsy and said, "You're still cancer-free."

After gaining victory over cancer, I was suddenly encouraging others to be overcomers by the grace of God. Around the Christmas season of 2014, a friend of mine had a serious cancer issue that flared up again and led to a major operation during that time. I said to her, "I've got to get you this book by Gregory Dixon." This is the best book I ever read. I gave her my only copy of *Christ Our Healer: A Revelation of Mercy* and said, "I can't do without this book." I got my second copy as soon as I could. It's the book that made the difference for me!

Just as I did, I encourage you to read this book over and over again until the principles truly take hold of your life. What God did for me, he can also do for you, because He is a God of great mercy and compassion!

—Daniel Kelly
Programmer Analyst Level III
Gettysburg, PA

ABOUT F. F. BOSWORTH

Fred Francis Bosworth (1877-1958) was one of the pioneers of the divine healing message who revolutionized the lives of millions over several decades with his sound biblical answers to controversial questions. Bosworth strongly influenced many Christian leaders and he was an advisor to many of the early healing revivalists such as William Branham, Oral Roberts, T.L. Osborn, and many others. He embraced Pentecostalism as a result of being influenced by Charles Parham in 1906. Around 1907, Bosworth along with John G. Lake visited the Azusa Street Revival and made contacts there. One photo shows them with William J. Seymour, the black Pentecostal preacher who led the Azusa Street Revival. The late Kenneth E. Hagin constantly referred to Bosworth's teachings, and many of the modern faith teachers draw from his outstanding teachings on divine healing today.

Bosworth worked with John Alexander Dowie for a number of years before starting his own healing ministry. Bosworth was also influenced by E.W. Kenyon and his teachings on divine healing. Bosworth's reputation spread rapidly throughout the 1920s as a result of a number of healing campaigns that he held throughout North America and Canada.

Christ the Healer, the book that Bosworth first published in 1924, and The National Radio Revival Missionary Crusaders ministry that he established had a far-reaching impact on countless lives. The first edition of *Christ the Healer* was simply a collection of his sermons on the topic of divine healing, along with theologically sound responses to his critics. Bosworth's ministry received more than 225,000 letters from people who testified of the divine healings and other blessings that they received based on his teachings, which inspired their faith. The remarkable results of his awesome ministry are proof that the Word of God has transforming power when properly applied by those who are sufficiently enlightened.

Fred Francis Bosworth was born on a farm near Utica, Nebraska, on January 17, 1877, and was raised in a Methodist home. At the age of 17, a friend from Omaha invited Fred to a three-day revival meeting at the First Methodist Church. On the third night that Fred attended the meetings, he went to the altar, repented of his sins and committed his life to Christ. A couple of years later, young Fred Bosworth contracted a severe cold that developed into serious lung trouble. His condition eventually grew so severe that his physician predicted that death was near. On a final trip he took to Fitzgerald, Georgia, to see his parents before his anticipated death, he drifted into a Methodist church where Miss Mattie Perry and others were conducting a series of meetings for the deepening of the spiritual life. "Fred coughed painfully all through the service and at its close went to the front to be prayed for with others who wanted more of God," explained Bosworth biographer Eunice M. Perkins. "Miss Perry told him how lovingly ready God was to make him well, in the name of Jesus, and laying her hands on him she prayed that he might be healed. From that self-same hour Fred began to mend, until, ere many days, his lung trouble was entirely a thing of the past."

When Fred Bosworth was 23, he met Miss Estella Hayde and married her while she was 18. A year or so later, he went to Zion City and began to play his cornet in John Alexander Dowie's church, where he was quickly promoted to band director.

Bosworth eventually took a step of faith and launched out on his own in full-time ministry as a traveling evangelist with no financial backing. He started his first church in Dallas in 1910. He was one of the founders of the Assemblies of God in 1914 and was with them until 1918. Most of his later ministry, however, was associated with the Christian and Missionary Alliance church.

In his early years of ministry, Bosworth experienced his share of trials and tragedies. His young son died on his fourth birthday, and several years later (in 1919) his wife also died. The Lord did bless Fred Bosworth to remarry later on.

In the 1921 edition of the book entitled *Joybringer Bosworth: His Life Story*, Bosworth biographer Eunice M. Perkins explained that Bosworth's first wife was a wonderful Christian who fell into the temptation of working herself to death:

> *Influenza, terminating in tuberculosis of the lungs, had attacked Mrs. Bosworth, who had been yielding for many*

years to the great temptation, always present, to overwork, until it had become such a fixed habit in her life as to make her an easy victim of disease. Repeatedly, the Lord had healed her; yet, repeatedly, she would succumb to the tendency to go beyond His will and her strength, until it seemed best to Him to call her, tho still a young woman, Home to Himself.

...She was joyfully ready to go, but her great gain, in departing to be with Christ, was bitter loss to her husband and their two, now motherless, daughters...overwork is at the root of a large percentage of the sorrow and suffering in this great country of ours. And the man or woman in Christ's service sees so much to be done and so few to do it, in this fact lies his or her temptation.

For, to be occupied with Himself, rather than with His work, will keep us in His order. Often, then, amidst the fuss and fever of multitudinous activities, we shall hear Him whisper to us, "Do not forget, My child, that My yoke is easy, My burden is light." A yoke that is rough and hard, and a burden that is heavy is always Satan-imposed or self-imposed.

This account is an example to every Christian that we must not allow our good intentions to serve God to go to unhealthy extremes. We must strive to be health-conscious and to live a balanced life, or we can open up the door to fatal sickness or disease.

Bosworth's healing ministry experienced a monumental change during a series of meetings in Lima, Ohio, in August 1920, about a year after his wife passed away. The fact that Bosworth had lost members of his own family could have shaken his faith concerning divine healing. But he decided not to base the truth of God's Word on the tragedies he experienced in his past. In Lima, Bosworth felt a special charge to preach on the subject of divine healing.

Feeling unsettled about the lack of understanding in the universal church regarding the subject of divine healing, Bosworth discussed the matter one night until far into the morning with his younger brother, Burton B. Bosworth. The question arose, "But what if sick folk are invited to come to the meetings to be prayed for in the name of Jesus and none of them get healed?" The answer was, "That would not be so disastrous as for sinners to come and go away without being saved.

The teaching of God's Word is plain and the people must be thus instructed. 'Faith cometh by hearing,' and while all may, some will hear, have faith and be healed."

From that point on the Lord made it plain for Bosworth to see, *If people didn't get saved, you wouldn't stop preaching the Gospel. In the same manner, if you preach on healing and the people come and don't get healed, you wouldn't stop preaching the healing message.*

While Bosworth had previously preached divine healing as the privilege of every child of God, an intensely focused study of the Bible on the subject of healing caused his understanding to be illuminated at a new level. His fresh revelation of an old truth inspired him to preach healing with a greater conviction, declaring that sick people, both saints and sinners, should be invited from far and near to hear what the compassionate Christ longs to do for their pain-racked bodies, as well as for their sin-burdened souls. More than ever before, Bosworth saw that it was God's will to heal as well as save people, and he had an encounter at that point and time that inspired him to teach, preach, and believe the healing message without reservation.

In the Lima meetings Bosworth made the unqualified proclamation that healing for the body is as truly a part of the Gospel as is salvation for the soul. He invited the sick to come and hear the word of healing for their bodies. The people responded, God then began to do a tremendous work and many were healed. The momentum of God's move continued throughout the 1920s and Bosworth was known for his "big tent revival" and large auditorium meetings and his advocacy of faith healing, with people from all denominations attending.

In his meetings, many people received miracles from the Lord, and many people were also known to be healed of deafness. David Du Plessis reported being in a Bosworth meeting in 1928, in which several students from a deaf school attended. Du Plessis witnessed Bosworth praying for each deaf child, and marvelled as all of them were miraculously healed and began hearing perfectly. The school for the deaf had to shut down their operation after the meeting because all of their students were healed.

After establishing The National Radio Revival Missionary Crusaders as a nonprofit corporation in Illinois, Bosworth was broadcasting regularly on WJJD and other radio stations in the Chicago area in the 1930s. Apparently, he was broadcasting from several stations across the country at one point and time, and he continued to broadcast well into the 1940s.

During the 1930s and 1940s, he also conducted many healing campaigns all over North America. In 1947 he met William Branham, who was just starting his ministry, and Bosworth became an advisor and mentor to Branham, T.L. Osborn, to a young Oral Roberts, and to other ministers. Bosworth prayed for the sick in many of Branham's meetings. He also ministered with Branham and others in Africa and Japan, and as of 1950, Fred Francis Bosworth commented that he had more than 30 years of great evangelistic campaigns, and 14 years of this time conducted the National Radio Revival, during which time he received about a quarter of a million letters.

In 1954 a 77-year-old F. F. Bosworth returned to Chicago and preached a message entitled "Be Ye Doers of the Word." In his message he emphasized the importance of acting on the Word as an act of faith. In other words, if you are feeling sick, you might get up and start walking around as a sign of faith. Then God's healing power begins to work in you all the more because of your faith in action. He shared a testimony of a time when he went out on the platform to preach in spite of feeling sick and received his healing. By sharing some testimonies of the miracles many received at his crusades in Africa, Bosworth also taught about the necessity for individuals to learn to receive healings through their own faith and prayers:

> *In Africa, thousands were healed of all manner of diseases, and thousands more saved as a result, and nearly all of them healed through their own prayer. Teaching them carefully and thoroughly so that all doubt could be removed about God's will, and then form a prayer for them, and while they prayed the mass prayer, God healed their bodies...[of] cancer...and everything including leprosy. I'm not telling you anything I did. I just reversed that idea all together. And told the people that I don't want anyone to base your faith on my faith, but to see that God wants to hear your own prayer. Every child of God found his place in the family. And like every baby can do his own crying, so how much more will our Heavenly Father hear those that cry to Him.*

Just that realization...There must be in your own mind from the Scriptures, the positive knowledge that it's God will, not that God can—that's no basis for faith—but that God will heal either the soul or the body...

We were simply amazed in Africa to see the Zulus and the Hindus and the Mohameders converted the very first service because of what they saw. And how they'd come to God in great groups, hundreds and hundreds at a time...different ones each night, coming with cancer alone and the same with the other diseases...we healed nobody, we gave no treatments...we taught them the Word and removed all the questions from their minds and then had them pray and God hear their prayer and heal their bodies...

After decades of ministry, in 1958, F. F. Bosworth told his family that it was time for him to go to heaven because the Lord had impressed upon him that he had "finished his course." His granddaughter states that Bosworth was disappointed the next morning when he woke up and was still alive on earth rather than in heaven.

He had not been diagnosed with any life-threatening sickness or disease, but he emphatically told his friends and loved ones that he would be going to meet the Lord in heaven at any time. As various ministers and friends got the news of Bosworth's anticipated departure, they rushed to visit him in order to say a final goodbye.

T.L. Osborn recalls going to Bosworth's house and hearing him shout, "Brother T.L.! This is the greatest day of my life! God has told me I get to go Home to be with Him today! Whooo! Hallelujah!"

In the final moments of his life, friends and family members were at his bedside as Bosworth opened his eyes to heaven and described the glories he was seeing. Without any sickness or disease, he passed away a few hours later. He was 81 years old and he peacefully went to sleep to spend eternity with his Lord and Savior Jesus Christ.

A GOD-INSPIRED BOOK

Thank God for the day I ran into Cheryl Lehmann for the very first time at a bookstore a number of years ago. She shared with me her testimony, telling me how she could have been dead from cancer, but God had healed her, thanks in part to the inspiration and knowledge that she had gained from reading *Christ the Healer* by F. F. Bosworth. This was my introduction to Bosworth's revolutionary book, which was first published in 1924.

When I first read *Christ the Healer*, it confirmed many ideas and answered many questions that I had formulated in my mind. The book is based on the idea that God is full of compassion and mercy and desires to heal all who are sick. (Bosworth, a very balanced communicator of the Word, also made it very clear that the salvation of the soul was more important than the healing of the body.) The bottom line, the book teaches, is that the Scriptures clearly show us that, concerning healing others, Jesus never lost a case and never denied anyone who had the faith to be healed. In fact, the only time Jesus couldn't do miracles was because of the individuals' unbelief **(see Matthew 13:58).**

The book that you are now reading was inspired by many of the things that I learned from studying the life and teachings of F. F. Bosworth, as well as the knowledge that I have gained from the Word of God and from other contemporary ministers. I am deeply inspired by Bosworth because his life and ministry represented what he taught. Countless thousands were healed through his ministry, and in 1958 even Bosworth himself died peacefully and without any sickness at the age of 81 because of his faith in Christ the healer. Bosworth's ministry received more than 225,000 letters from people who testified of divine healings and other blessings that they had received based on his teachings, which inspired their faith. Obviously, if Bosworth's ministry received nearly a quarter-million letters, then there were no doubt thousands or even millions of others who never wrote in to testify of the miraculous healings that they experienced as a result of Bosworth's fruitful ministry.

Years before being introduced to Bosworth's book, the Lord had been dealing with me personally about the great depth of his mercy in all areas of my life. Considering some of my personal failures, I knew that I should have gone under in many ways. But I pleaded with the Lord for mercy, and I actually saw God give me many good things that I did not deserve in the midst of some of my worst failures. From firsthand experience I got a real revelation of the Lord's mercy and grace.

This is not to imply that one should continuously or willfully commit sin and take advantage of God's grace, because the Lord is not mocked. **"Shall we continue in sin, that grace may abound? God forbid" (Romans 6:1-2).** Rather, in the midst of my personal failures I simply cried out to the Lord with a sincere heart, asking him to show me mercy. Based on what David said in **Psalm 103**, I pleaded with the Lord that he would not deal with me after my sins or reward me according to my iniquities. And I am convinced that, although I suffered negative consequences for my actions, the Lord showed me great mercy by allowing me to escape much of the penalty I deserved. Furthermore, I gained a greater understanding of the fact that we are all products of the Lord's mercy.

I believe that the principles related to God's mercy that are contained in this book will give the sick a revelation that will stir them to a greater trust in the mercy of God as it applies to the healing of the body and soul.

Has Jesus stopped doing what he did in the four Gospels and in the book of Acts—healing all who come to him in faith? If Jesus has changed, then should we not take Hebrews 13:8 out of the Holy Bible?

Hebrews 13:8 (NKJV)
Jesus Christ is the same yesterday, today, and forever.

If Jesus is the same today as he was yesterday, then why are so many theologians trying to explain away the Lord's desire to heal the sick in our day and time? The Bible admonishes us to teach the whole counsel of God. **In Acts 20:27, Paul the Apostle declared, "For I have not shunned to declare unto you all the counsel of God."** If we are teaching the full counsel of God, we ought not to disregard his words on healing.

In his book *Christ the Healer*, Fred Francis Bosworth declared:

> *The reason why many of the sick in our day have not returned to their physical possessions is that they have not heard the trumpet sound concerning healing. "Faith cometh by hearing," and they have not heard because many ministers had their Gospel put out of order while in the theological seminary.*

As Bosworth pointed out, some people attempt to theologically justify man's failure to be healed as God's failure to heal. There are others who will theologically justify the premature death of our precious young saints who died from sickness rather than obey the biblical command to pray **"the prayer of faith" that will save the sick (James 5:14-15)**. John Wesley, the great Methodist minister, declared that once upon a time the Christian church followed the command to pray the prayer of faith as the number one means for healing the sick until doubt and unbelief came in.

In spite of the wonderful Christians I know who would attempt to theologically justify the "premature death" of many good Christian people who died of diseases, I have never accepted those individuals' illnesses and resulting deaths as God's will based on what I have read in the four Gospels and in the book of Acts.

The question I would like to pose to you is this: "Whose report shall you believe?" Will you trust in man's faulty theology or the infallible Word of God regarding the truth about divine healing? Bosworth boldly declared,

> *I, for one, will preach all the Gospel if I never see another man saved or healed as long as I live. I am determined to base my doctrines on the immutable word of God, not on phenomena or human experience.*

Bosworth was so radical about following God's principles for divine healing that he boldly declared that he would base his faith only on God's Word. **Bosworth declared that even if he prayed for**

a sick person and that person dropped dead, he would step over his or her dead body and pray for the next person!

Get radical about receiving your healing and *touch the hem of Christ's garment so that you can be made whole.* As F. F. Bosworth put it so eloquently,

> *You cannot touch him with reservation. Like the woman who pressed through the throng and touched Him, you must "elbow" selfishness, disobedience, unconfessed sins, lukewarmness, public opinion, traditions of men, and articles written against divine healing out of your way. In fact you must often press beyond your own pastor, who may be unenlightened in this part of the Gospel. Press beyond doubts, doublemindedness, symptoms, feelings, and the lying Serpent.*

How to Use This Book

The book that you are now reading is intended to be a brief guide that will give you modern-day testimonies to stir your faith along with biblical principles and Scriptures that you can read over and over again for the healing of the body. It is designed as a powerful, short and quick reference tool to help you to understand and apply the biblical principles of divine healing. In it I have broken down Bosworth's awesome teaching into 10 powerful principles that will revolutionize your faith.

One purpose for this book is to open up the windows of opportunity for many more to be healed by enlightening the readers with the simple knowledge that God is not only able to heal us, but God desires to heal us. And we are in a much better place to receive healing from God if we will take Him at his Word and apply His Word. If I can accomplish this basic purpose, then I will feel that I have accomplished something very much worthwhile.

I once heard Pastor Kerry Kirkwood say, "In order to shrink the problem, you've got to magnify the solution." And this book, designed to be read and meditated upon over and over again, is a great tool for helping the reader to magnify God and His healing virtues.

I also highly recommend that you read Bosworth's original edition of *Christ the Healer* in its entirety in order to give you even greater understanding about divine healing and also to stir your faith with the awesome testimonies of healings that took place as a result of Bosworth's ministry. In my opinion it is one of the best, most balanced, and most thorough books available on the subject of divine healing, even though Bosworth wrote the first edition of the book back in 1924.

It has been decades since Bosworth wrote the first edition and the book is still in print. The special ninth edition of the book published by Revell (a division of Baker Book House Company) also has an excellent forward written by Robert V. Bosworth, son of F. F. Bosworth, along with additional sections not contained in the original 1924 book. The sections have titles such as "Why Some Fail To Receive Healing" and "The Ultimate Triumph" (a section about how Bosworth was miraculously healed himself, how his ministry impacted countless thousands, and how he died peacefully; it is written by his son Robert).

Bosworth was not a perfect vessel, but according to my assessment he was a very balanced theologian regarding the doctrine of divine healing, and he exalted the Word of God above human experiences and traditions of men. Even though he suffered tragedies and setbacks in his own life and ministry, he did not allow these unfortunate experiences to cause him to abandon his faith or discredit the Word of God. From reading his book about faith and divine healing, you will see that Bosworth did his homework and was not merely expressing man's opinions but communicating unchanging principles from the Word of God.

I believe that by reading Bosworth's extremely thorough exposition of *Christ the Healer* along with studying this condensed reference tool, you will make remarkable progress in terms of understanding and utilizing your faith properly. And for those who don't have as much time on their hands to read initially, this shorter reference tool alone is a great start on the pathway of understanding faith and divine healing according to the Word of God.

If you are sick and in need of healing, use this book as a guide to pray according to the Scriptures that are contained in this book. Read the principles contained in this book over and over again, and act on them as well.

When using this book to minister to others, read select portions out loud, and encourage the sick to read and pray the Scriptures and principles that are contained in this book. If they are not capable of reading for themselves, then you can read to them until the word takes root, for **"faith cometh by hearing, and hearing by the word of God" (Romans 10:17).**

Although the primary focus of this book is related to Christ's atonement for physical healing, you can also apply the principles in this book to obtain healing for the body and soul. Christ heals physical diseases, broken-heartedness, emotional trauma, mental devastation, deep sorrow, and sin-sickness. **Psalm 41:4 says, "Lord, be merciful to me; Heal my soul, for I have sinned against you"** (NKJV).

It's Supernatural

The Lord blessed me to write this book supernaturally by the guidance of the Holy Spirit. This is also the first book written that breaks Bosworth's teachings down into 10 principles that make his insights on divine healing even easier to understand and apply. Furthermore, the way the teachings of F. F. Bosworth are broken down into 10 principles in this book was given to me directly from the Lord.

One reason I felt the need to write this book was because of the great need to dispel many of the erroneous concepts related to the subject of divine healing. Based on my reading of the New Testament, I could not find one instance where Jesus refused to heal anyone who came to him in faith. The bottom line is that in the New Testament Scriptures, Jesus never lost a case! As previously mentioned, the only times he did not heal people was because of their own unbelief and not because of the Lord's refusal to heal them. But aside from unbelief, there are other reasons individuals don't get healed. This book will show you through scriptural evidence that Jesus healed all who met his conditions and came to him in faith. And through the sharing of 10 principles, this book will also show you how to deal with issues that can hinder the healing power of God.

I also want to point out to you from the very beginning that it is not my intent to judge Christians who do not get healed for one reason or another. My main objective is to help Christians to avoid missing out on God's best concerning the healing of the body and soul. Scripture verses like **1 Corinthians 11:30** clearly teach that there are some Christians who get sick and die before their time due to sin or disobedience. In the case of the blind man in **John 9:1-3**, however, Jesus pointed out that the man's blindness was not necessarily because of any act of disobedience or personal sin in the life of the blind man, his mother, or his father. In other words, if a person is sick, it is not necessarily the result of sin in his or her life, although this could be the case.

"And as Jesus passed by, he saw a man which was blind from his birth. And his disciples asked him, saying, Master, who did sin, this man, or his parents, that he was born blind? Jesus answered, Neither hath this man sinned, nor his parents: but that the works of God should be made manifest in him" (John 9:1-3).

In other words, our limited human understanding will not always know why a person is handicapped or sick. And Jesus healed the man that was born blind in order to reveal the works of God, His healing power. This reminds us that another purpose for supernatural healing is to glorify God by setting Christ and Christianity apart from other vain or powerless religions. Rather than speculate or seek man's opinion as to why a person is sick, it is better to ask God what he wants us to see in order to remove any possible hindrances to healing.

Scriptures like **1 Thessalonians 4:13** also teach us that if a person who dies is truly saved, then we should not **"sorrow as others who have no hope."** Consequently, even if a true child of God dies of sickness, we need to look at their death from God's perspective. **Psalm 116:15 says, "Precious in the sight of the LORD is the death of his saints."** Philippians 1:21-23 lets us know that those who go home to meet the Lord are in a better place than those of us who remain on this earth. **"For to me to live is Christ, and to die is gain," said the Apostle Paul in Philippians 1:21.** In his time of great persecution, Paul was facing the possibility of being put to death for preaching the gospel, so he was torn between the ideas of staying alive a bit longer to lead more souls to Christ or being put to death to experience the glory of being with the Lord for all eternity. **"For I am hard-pressed between the two, having a desire to depart and be with Christ, which is far better,"** Paul said in Philippians 1:23 (NKJV). In 2 Corinthians 5:8, the Apostle Paul also said, **"We are confident, I say, and willing rather to be absent from the body, and to be present with the Lord."**

Because the glory of heaven and the misery of hell are real and the Bible teaches that every person will spend eternity in either place, your salvation and your relationship with Christ should always be first and foremost above seeking physical healing. Salvation through Christ is the greatest miracle. Consequently, the first thing I would admonish any reader to do is to get right with God if necessary. Although our Sovereign Lord sometimes chooses to heal those who are not saved, as we will later see through the testimony of Nasir Siddiki, the Scripture teaches us that it is necessary to get right with God to be assured that the Lord will hear our prayers. So before a person begins praying for a physical healing, I would suggest that the individual ask the Lord to save his or her soul first and foremost. **Isaiah 59:1-2 says, "Behold, the LORD'S hand is not shortened, that it cannot save; neither his ear heavy, that it cannot hear: But your iniquities have separated between you and your God, and your sins have hid his face from you, that he will not hear."** These verses let us know that our sins can prevent God from hearing our prayers, but the Lord is ready to save us and hear us whenever we are ready to repent.

Consequently, you must make sure that you are absolutely certain of your salvation in order to get the proper benefits from this book. You need to totally surrender your life to Christ if you have not done so already. Consider the following Scriptures that relate to how any person can receive salvation through Christ:

Romans 10:9 (NKJV)
That if you confess with your mouth the Lord Jesus and believe in your heart that God has raised Him from the dead, you will be saved.

Romans 10:13 (NKJV)
For whoever calls on the name of the Lord shall be saved.

Acts 4:12 (NKJV)
Nor is there salvation in any other, for there is no other name under heaven given among men by which we must be saved.

According to the above Scriptures, all you need to do is believe that Jesus Christ (the Son of God) proved His divinity when He rose from the dead, believe that He is the only way to salvation, and call on Him by asking Him to save you and forgive you of your sins. Perhaps you have done this already, but I don't want to assume anything, so I am sharing this information with you because I am more concerned about your eternal salvation than I am about your physical healing.

The Enemy's Greatest Weapon

Before I begin sharing the true-life testimonies and the teachings of F. F. Bosworth, I would like to share with you some basic principles concerning Satan's greatest weapon.

What is the enemy's greatest weapon for causing individuals to go to hell or to miss out on the promises of God?

The answer—a lie.

Jesus told the religious hypocrites, **"Ye are of your father the devil, and the lusts of your father ye will do. He was a murderer from the beginning, and abode not in the truth, because there is no truth in him. When he speaketh a lie, he speaketh of his own: for he is a liar, and the father of it (John 8:44)."**

Jesus was letting us know that Satan's greatest weapon is a lie. If Satan can keep people ignorant of God's truth, he can keep them sick and depressed and even lead them to hell. **Isaiah 5:13-14** further confirms this by letting us know that hell has enlarged itself because of ignorance.

William James, the father of modern psychology, said, "There is nothing so absurd, but if you repeat it often enough people will believe it." In other words, if you take even the most outlandish lie and repeat it enough, people will believe it. Adolf Hitler, like William James, recognized the power of repetition in getting people to believe lies.

If Satan can lie to sinners to keep them from receiving salvation through Christ, he can certainly lie to Christians to keep them from receiving healing through Christ.

To illustrate my point further, consider this basic question: *Because of Christ's atonement, is salvation of the soul available to everyone who will call on Christ in faith?* The answer is obviously *yes*, because Romans 10:13 declares, "For whosoever shall call upon the name of the Lord shall be saved."

Because everyone will not call upon the name of the Lord for the salvation of the soul, however, everyone will not receive salvation although Jesus paid the price for all.

The insight we can gain from this point can also be related to the concept of divine healing. Although Isaiah 53:5 and other Scriptures let us know that healing is made available to everyone through the atonement, everyone will not reach out to receive it by faith. And one of the primary reasons some will not reach out to receive healing through Christ is because Satan will lie to them, telling them that God wants to glorify himself by keeping them sick. Some Christians will believe this although Christ never said anything like this.

This entire book is focused on giving you God's Word regarding his desire to heal all who will be obedient to him and meet his conditions. Since the Scriptures below let us know that God cannot lie, it would benefit us to learn what his Word says regarding physical healing so that we can apply it to our lives and receive the full benefits of God's promises.

God Cannot Lie

Hebrews 6:18 (NKJV)
… it is impossible for God to lie …

Titus 1:2
In hope of eternal life, which God, that cannot lie, promised before the world began…

Romans 3:3-4
For what if some did not believe? shall their unbelief make the faith of God without effect? God forbid: yea, let God be true, but every man a liar…

Numbers 23:19
God is not a man, that he should lie; neither the son of man, that he should repent: hath he said, and shall he not do it? or hath he spoken, and shall he not make it good?

AMAZING TRUE-LIFE TESTIMONIES OF INDIVIDUALS WHO WERE HEALED AND INFLUENCED BY THE TEACHINGS OF F. F. BOSWORTH

The four contemporary testimonies that you are about to read are all from individuals who are presently living and were all impacted by the teachings of F. F. Bosworth, either directly from Bosworth's book or indirectly from a minister who was influenced by Bosworth's teachings.

Bosworth had a great influence on many of the early healing evangelists, such as Oral Roberts, T.L. Osborn, John G. Lake, Kenneth Hagin, Sr., and others. Many of our contemporary healing evangelists, such as Kenneth and Gloria Copeland, Nasir Siddiki, and Benny Hinn, have also been impacted by reading *Christ the Healer* or by early healing evangelists who have passed on Bosworth's teachings. It is awesome to know that the influence of Bosworth's teaching is still leading individuals to the healing power of Christ more than ninety years after he first wrote *Christ the Healer*!

Cheryl Lehmann
Victory over Cancer

As I stated in the introduction to this book, I met Cheryl Lehmann (pronounced "Lay-man") for the very first time in the year 2004 while I was in a bookstore. She shared with me her testimony, telling me of how she could have been dead from cancer, but God had healed her, thanks in part to the inspiration and knowledge that she had gained from reading *Christ the Healer* by F.F. Bosworth. And that was my introduction to Bosworth's revolutionary book, which was first published in 1924.

Cheryl Lehmann has read *Christ the Healer* more than a dozen times. She says it is her favorite book to recommend to those who have been diagnosed with cancer. When Cheryl first learned about the book in 1999, she was in desperate need of healing. The doctors had already told her that she only had two months left to live unless she took chemotherapy. And even after receiving the chemotherapy, she was told that she had only two years to live at most. But *Christ the Healer* helped to elevate Cheryl's faith and trust in God for healing and ultimately brought healing to her body.

"The book was like a good dessert," she says. "I couldn't stop reading it, and I was always finding answers for my future. I learned that the Word works. I read the four Gospels over and over again, and I couldn't find in any one of them where Jesus said, 'I won't heal you,' if the person came to him in faith. But there was always something they were required to do."

Cheryl says that if she discerns that others are eager to know the biblical principles for divine healing, she does not hesitate to buy them a copy of *Christ the Healer*. For those who will put aside laziness and are serious about doing whatever it takes to be healed, "it is a good investment," she says. "But I have also discovered that sometimes people just want to say things like, 'Pray for me so that I can get better,' but they don't want to do anything on their own. If we are willing to do what it takes, we can rebuild our temples with the Word of God and proper nutrition."

Cheryl was first diagnosed with a form of cancer referred to as non-Hodgkin's lymphoma in 1994. A biopsy of a salivary gland confirmed that the cancer was confined to that location, and she initially received six months of chemotherapy. The cancer took a serious toll on her body. "I had a lump come out on the side of my head," she explains. "The doctors didn't know what to do with it. It was a frightening thing above my ear where people could see it. Also, a big lump almost the size of a fist came out the back of my head. The cancer also started to grow around organs internally."

She went to many prayer meetings related to healing. "Every time someone prayed for me I'd reach to feel if the lump was going down to see if the prayer had been effective. I was walking by sight and getting disgusted because I felt that the prayer meetings weren't working."

From 1994 to 1999 the cancer got progressively worse. Throughout her ordeal, it seemed that new tumors appeared every 2 ½ to 3 years. The tumors appeared in various organs and in several different areas of her body, including the groin area, axilla, clavicle area, the back of her head, the center of her back, and several times on her left thigh. As a registered nurse, Cheryl detested taking chemotherapy, so in 1998, she went to a Christian-based clinic in Tijuana, Mexico, hoping for less toxicity.

All through the journey, she relied on the prayers of friends and her own strong faith, which was challenged frequently. Eventually the chemotherapy became so severe that the doctors began preparing her for a stem cell transplant. But Cheryl was rejected by Johns Hopkins Hospital for the transplant, because they believed "it would kill her" due to consistently low blood counts.

This was during her darkest hour in 1999. The doctors had told her that she could not take chemotherapy anymore, had no other alternative, and only had two years to live at the most, because the disease had manifested itself in so many locations. Fortunately, this was also around the time that she had acquired Bosworth's revolutionary book.

Up to that point, Cheryl had been a Christian for many years but did not have knowledge of the principles presented by Bosworth in his book. She would simply look up the Scriptures on healing and hope that something good would happen. But she says that reading Bosworth's book "gave the assurance that healing is for everyone, but you just have to boldly claim it."

In spite of the physical damage that had already been done to her body due to the cancer, Cheryl discovered Bosworth's book and learned how to exercise her faith and extend her life beyond the predictions of her doctors. Eventually, with the help of the doctors and prayer, the lumps started to drain and dissolve. Cheryl explains that before she read *Christ the Healer,* she had an enormous amount of fear even during the beginning stages of the cancer. After the book armed her with knowledge, however, she was later able to overcome fear during the more critical stage when she was told that she only had two months to live. She is a walking miracle and another testimony that the Lord still brings forth awesome deliverance.

In addition to using the book to help her identify hindrances related to her healing, Cheryl also says, "The book helped me to rely on the Lord's strength to uphold his Word rather than just my faith. If I had never gotten Bosworth's book, I think I would be six feet under. But the book gave me a boldness to hold on to the Word and not cast away my confidence. Before reading the book, I would look at other minister- s' wives who had died of cancer and say, 'If they didn't have the faith, then what's going to happen to me?'

"I would also look at rich people like Jacqueline Kennedy Onassis, who couldn't get delivered from cancer in spite of great financial resources. Onassis was diagnosed with the same form of cancer (lymphoma) the same year that I was first diagnosed with it in 1994, and she died in 1997, the same year that my cancer came back with a fierce vengeance. So you can imagine how this opened me up to greater fear because I simply did not accept the Word at face value at that time.

"And everybody was always praying for me, 'If it be thy will, heal her.' Finally, I was able to say, 'It is God's will.' based on what I learned from Bosworth's book. I would say it is the best gift you can give any sick person who is terminally ill just because of the empha- sis on the Word."

It was 1999 when the doctors gave Cheryl Lehmann only two months to live. Now, because of *Christ the Healer*, she is still alive more than 15 years after that prediction! Instead of going to her grave prematurely, she is allowing the Lord to use her life to help others find deliverance from sickness and despair.

"After I got the book, I learned to believe before seeing," says Cheryl. "*Christ the Healer* was a big turning point for me, because after reading it I was no longer walking by sight or focusing on symp- toms. I now have to continue the faith walk in spite of challenges that require me to continue to gaze into the Lord's eyes with steadfast faith as Bosworth taught. I had to learn to totally walk by faith or life would have been miserable. But instead of living in misery I have the victory in Christ!

"I'm a nurse, so I'm taught to read reports and believe them. But in spite of the reports that told me I only had two months to live in

1999, I am living proof that Christ is the ultimate Healer. I am still in the land of the living by the grace of God. The Lord has given me a mission in life to help others to see the practical application of Scripture the same way that Bosworth helped me to see it. Bosworth put the supernatural back into God, which many of today's churches fail to accentuate. I have learned that the more you share the Word out loud and speak faith, the more your faith grows."

The knowledge Cheryl received from the Bible and from Bosworth's book was desperately needed in order to overcome the battle scars that had accumulated over the years. Because of liver damage caused by chemotherapy, Cheryl developed esophageal varices. These led to two emergency hospital admissions for internal bleeding, both of which occurred while she was away from home (the second time while on vacation in North Carolina). Radiation was now the treatment of choice for the next six tumors, and by the time the last series of tumors appeared on the left thigh (one the size of a small fist), the radiation oncologist said "no more radiation."

"That was in the spring of 2007, and we headed for our biannual beach vacation," says Cheryl. "I had learned about speaking to the mountain and commanded these tumors into the sea. I also studied about daily communion for healing purposes and made that a practice."

The tumors did not leave right away, but Cheryl says, "In the fall of 2007, I read an article in Sid Roth's magazine relaying the proof that all matter emits sound waves, and that those in cancerous tumors are morbid, dissonant sounds unlike those produced by other healthy tissues. Armed with this ammunition, I chose to play John Hagee's healing Scripture verses on CD through earphones clamped around the thigh tumors twice a day after praying and commanding these illegal growths to leave my body. In two weeks, the tumors were gone; the largest one leaving a raw area that healed in the shape of a heart on my thigh! Time and time again, God showed his faithfulness in caring for my every need in this long journey. I am, indeed, both humbled and grateful to have experienced His touch—an 'out of the box' miracle for me!"

Along with recommending Bosworth's original book to those who need to build faith for healing, Cheryl Lehmann also uses the book you are now reading as one of her primary tools for sharing the message of divine healing.

"Words can't express what I felt when I first read the book *Christ Our Healer: A Revelation of Mercy* by Greg Dixon," she says. "It far exceeded my expectations! Greg has done a marvelous job of condensing the essentials of healing principles from the original version, making it so much more user-friendly. I know so many lives will be rescued for the kingdom. Thanks, Greg, for all you are doing to make known the healing power of Jesus! The books are still doing the job that they were designed to do, so I want to have extra copies available whenever I can."

A member of the Christian Life Assembly Church (CLA) in Camp Hill, Pennsylvania, Cheryl Lehmann is presently a group leader for Victory Seekers—a cancer support group ministry of CLA. Cheryl chose the name "Victory Seekers" because she discovered that through Christ she had the ability to choose life or death. "Everybody dies at some point," she proclaims, "but as Christians we are called to a life of victory through Jesus on this earth before we go to heaven."

Oomen Family Testimony
Autistic Son Healed

Desmond Oomen is now a young man who is living a more fulfilling life because of the faith of his parents. When Adrie Oomen's son, Desmond, was about four years old, Adrie and his wife, Annet, sent Desmond to school for the first time. His parents noticed that at school he acted very strange and also did not make any friends like children typically do. Desmond's parents were especially concerned and alarmed when he did strange things like banging his head on the wall.

When Desmond was five years old, a psychologist diagnosed him with autism. The report said that the child had a "serious impairment related to autism. Desmond had a clear delay in the field of language, speech, motor skills, handling of materials and social skills." The doctors informed the Oomens that their child had been born with a condition that would cause him to be abnormal for the rest of his life.

Autism is a condition that is linked to the abnormal biological and neurochemical development of the brain. It is also classified as a neurodevelopmental disorder that manifests itself in markedly abnormal social interaction, communication ability, patterns of interest, and patterns of behavior. The condition can range from nearly dysfunctional to severely mentally handicapped.

In Desmond's case, the prognosis did not offer any hope for the future. The psychologist explained that Desmond was mentally impaired to the point that his parents did not need to make future plans for their son. Instead, they could only hope that he could grow up and live in a decent environment around other disadvantaged individuals like himself.

The Oomens faced the challenge of raising an autistic child in their home in Holland. The draining effort and the number of hours required to care for the child daily put an incredible strain on Adrie and Annet's marriage. They recall the situation as hell on earth, because the stress and overextension affected them to the point where they were at one another's throats and feeling miserable most of the time. It was a very grim and gloomy situation for Adrie and Annet Oomen, with very little light at the end of the tunnel.

Then one day Pastor Hans Oudhoff of Jubilee Breda, Holland, told Annet that God could heal her child. The pastor's comment made Annet angry, because it had already been three years since her son had been tested and diagnosed with autism, and she felt that the preacher was being a bit presumptuous or arrogant to assume that he knew better than the doctor. And if it was indeed true that the Lord could heal her son, then Annet wondered, "What have I done in the church all these years?"

The pastor gave Annet a tape by Gloria Copeland on the topic of healing. Like so many others in the ministry, Gloria and Kenneth Copeland were both influenced by the powerful teachings of F. F. Bosworth. Kenneth Copeland had travelled on healing crusades with Oral Roberts, and Oral Roberts obviously shared with the Copelands some of the divine healing insights he learned from his mentor, F. F. Bosworth. Annet, however, was still skeptical after Pastor Oudhoff gave her the Copeland tapes. She wondered how someone could possibly be healed by listening to a voice on a tape recorder.

She soon discovered, however, that it was the Word of God on the tapes that contained the power. She discovered that it was not about a faith movement or an American fad or anything like that, but it was simply God's Word that brought hope for her autistic son. Annet couldn't stop listening because she was entirely consumed—

captivated—by the Word of God. The tape she listened to also helped to wipe away all her arguments as to why Desmond couldn't be healed. She began to understand the power in the Word of God when it is properly applied. "Faith cometh by hearing, and hearing by the word of God" (Romans 10:17). It spite of seemingly hopeless circumstances, the Oomens spoke the Word of God over their situation and trusted the Lord to heal their son.

Pastor Oudhoff also encouraged Annet, telling her that Desmond would do well in school and would eventually become whatever he wanted to become. At the moment, however, the situation didn't seem as hopeful. Desmond couldn't catch a ball and couldn't ride a bike, except with special training wheels, at ages seven and eight. Nevertheless, his mother resisted the temptation to give in to the symptoms of his illness and started speaking positively and thanking God. She began making statements like, "I believe this will be a great man of God who will do great things in the future." As a means of focusing on the Word of God, she had her son repeat healing Scriptures.

One day two years later, Desmond came to Annet and asked her why she had put him in a school with all those strange children. Annet was amazed at this comment, because for the first time her son seemed to notice that something was abnormal about the other autistic children. He was asking her why they didn't look at or talk to each other and why they shook on the floor or did other strange things. Annet was amazed that her child was speaking like a normal kid. God had manifested his healing!

Adrie was also amazed when he came home to a different Desmond. To Adrie's amazement, Desmond was acting, looking, and talking like any other normal child. Desmond was healed of autism! Through this experience, Adrie learned that once we know that the Word of God is true, we should "just do it." Do what the Word says even if it seems unusual.

Now a young man who is sharing his faith with others, Desmond says that when he was healed the ropes of his illness were cut off of him like a puppet's strings. He was no longer controlled by autism but was set free by Christ the Healer.

It was spectacular, and it was also a testament that "all things are possible to him that believeth" (Mark 9:23)! Desmond also says that he is aware that he must continue to walk in obedience to God's principles so that he doesn't lose the blessing of the healing that the Lord has granted him.

Annet says that God "turned our 'mourning into dancing' (Psalm 30:11)." And Desmond explains that he knows why he chooses God above everything else: He knows that his future will be good as long as he stays on the path with God!

Nasir and Anita Siddiki
A Muslim Healed of Shingles and His Wife Healed of Multiple Sclerosis

I first met my friend Nasir Siddiki along with his lovely wife, Anita, several years ago in Tulsa, Oklahoma, where they reside. I was helping him to produce some literature in the beginning stages of his ministry. As I helped him to communicate his ministry purpose through printed literature, Nasir shared with me everything about his conversion experience, his healing, his business background, and his ministry endeavors. Based on what I learned, it was obvious to me that God was going to elevate him in a splendid fashion over time.

At that time, Nasir and his wife were recent graduates of Bible school and had recently started Wisdom Ministries. They both had been miraculously healed from incurable diseases. Nasir was a former Muslim with an amazing testimony of the salvation and healing power of Christ. And, most of all, Nasir and Anita had a great sense of integrity along with a deep dedication and love for their Lord and Savior, Jesus Christ. I did not have to be a rocket scientist to figure out that there were many great things in store for the future of this progressive, God-fearing couple, and I felt it was an honor and a privilege to help them promote their mission. Now, when I watch Nasir on many of the top television ministries or other programs, it is absolutely no surprise to me to see how God is using him at the next level. But to better understand why God is using Nasir and Anita Siddiki in such a marvelous fashion, we must go back to the point when Nasir did not know Christ as Savior or Healer.

Before his dramatic conversion experience, Nasir was a highly successful Muslim businessman by the world's standards. He raised millions of dollars in revenue for companies worldwide and attracted thousands as a seminar speaker. But one day he was suddenly diagnosed with shingles—a deadly virus that attacked his nervous system. At the height of his career, Nasir was relegated to a hospital bed with grotesque blisters all over his face and body. The most frightening moment of all came when Nasir heard his doctors say that he was going to die.

The doctors, thinking Nasir was unconscious, did not realize that he could actually hear them talking about his condition. As Nasir was helplessly dying from an incurable disease, he cried out in desperation, "God, if you're real, don't let me die!" Nasir admits that at that time he did not believe in Jesus as the Son of God, but he also did not believe that his Muslim god, Allah, was a healer. Though the desperate Muslim businessman did not understand many things about Christianity at that time, he says he knew that it was the God of the Christians who answered his cry. "It was not Muhammad. It was not Allah. It was Jesus who came for this dying Muslim. He saved me, healed me, delivered me, and set me free," Nasir proclaims.

The very next morning after Nasir cried out, the blisters stopped growing. After he was released from the hospital, Nasir got on his knees at home and asked Christ to come into his life. The fact that the Lord had healed him even before he became a Christian was a splen-did example of God's mercy. In a few days, all of the remaining blis-ters fell off Nasir's body as he spent much time reading the Bible.

He then shared his miraculous experience with his coworker, Anita, who was already a Christian. Nasir and Anita developed a deeper friendship and eventually got married. They had a beautiful honeymoon and were deeply in love.

About a year into their marriage, a major financial setback occurred that caused them to lose everything. Even worse, while Anita was four and a half months pregnant she suddenly became seri-ously ill. Her hands and feet twisted up, she became paralyzed from the neck down on the right side of her body, and she also went blind.

It was like a nightmare. But in spite of the circumstances, Nasir and his wife still trusted in the Lord. Nasir knew that if Christ was merciful enough to heal him while he was a Muslim who didn't have a real understanding of faith at the time, then the God of mercy would heal his believing wife.

The baby was born, but Anita could not enjoy her baby due to her severe illness. She was diagnosed with multiple sclerosis, and the doctors determined that she would be crippled for the rest of her life.

Anita knew that God was a healer and remembered what the Lord had done for Nasir even when he wasn't a true believer, but her paralyzed condition was trying to paralyze her faith. Consequently, Nasir knew that he had to help protect his wife from fear and doubt. To keep Anita focused on the Word of God, he bought a continuous-play tape recorder and played healing tapes by Kenneth Hagin day and night.

Hagin is another one of the many healing evangelists who was influenced by the teachings of F. F. Bosworth. In fact, when Nasir went to RHEMA Bible Training College, which was founded by Hagin, one of the courses Nasir took utilized *Christ the Healer* as required reading.

As Anita listened to the healing tapes over and over, she remained steadfast in faith. Her body began to improve more and more as the days went by, and two and a half years later she was fully cured of multiple sclerosis, with no trace of the disease left in her body! Now she is traveling around the world and teaching the principles of divine healing along with her husband.

Nasir Siddiki and his wife Anita are both proof that miracles have not passed away!

Principle
1

STARVE DOUBT
AND FEED FAITH
Read and Hear the Word Continually

Get seriously obsessed with learning the Word of God, especially as it applies to the area in which you need help—in this case, physical healing.

F. F. Bosworth taught that instead of just asking a minister to pray for us, it is more important for us to seek to be taught God's Word so that we can properly cooperate with God for our recovery.

Too many of God's people know more about trivial things like sports and entertainment than we do about the Word of God. When we get obsessed with seeking and finding the relevant principles of God's Word, we will find the help that we truly need. God's Word, if we know it and if we know how to apply it to our specific problems, is *health to our flesh. Those who are sick should continually meditate on the Scriptures that relate to healing and focus on the Word, not the symptoms of their illness.*

Proverbs 4:20-22
My son, attend to my words; incline thine ear unto my sayings. Let them not depart from thine eyes; keep them in the midst of thine heart. For they are life unto those that find them, and health to all their flesh.

Romans 10:17
So then faith cometh by hearing, and hearing by the word of God.

Hosea 4:6
My people are destroyed for lack of knowledge.

Romans 12:2
And be not conformed to this world: but be ye transformed by the renewing of your mind, that ye may prove what is that good, and acceptable, and perfect, will of God.

Psalm 119
This entire Psalm demonstrates David's obsessive commitment to continually feeding on the Word of God. The following are a few selections.

Thy word have I hid in mine heart (vs. 11).

I will meditate in thy precepts (vs. 15).

I will delight myself in thy statutes; I will not forget thy word (vs. 16).

So shall I keep thy law continually for ever and ever (vs. 44).

O how I love thy law! It is my meditation all the day (vs. 97).

Thy word is a lamp unto my feet, and a light unto my path (vs. 105).

I love thy commandments above gold (vs. 127).

I rejoice at thy word (vs. 162).

The Scriptures let us know that just as God wants to save the soul, he also wants to heal the body. But we must have our minds renewed by the Word of God so that we can understand his will more fully.

The devil can only do certain things to us if we open up the door through disobedience or ignorance. Satan likes to capitalize on a person's lack of understanding concerning the Word of God. When the devil tried to deceive Christ, he even used Scriptures out of context (see Matthew 4). But Jesus defeated the enemy by giving him the Word of God in proper context, saying, "It is written."

The Bible declares, **"My people are destroyed for lack of knowledge" (Hosea 4:6).** A lack of knowledge also causes a lack of faith, and **without faith it is impossible to please the Lord (see Hebrews 11:6).** Romans 12:3 declares that **"God hath dealt to every man the measure of faith."** Consequently, the question is not *do you have faith?* But the question is *do you use the faith that God has already given you?* God gives everyone "the" measure of faith, not "a" measure of faith. In other words, we all basically start off with the same measure of faith, but we must develop it. One way to develop it is to hear and speak the Word of God over and over again. With proper knowledge, we can gain the victory and build faith by saying, like Jesus, "It is written."

Since fear runs contrary to faith, we must speak the Word of God and rebuke all fear.

2 Timothy 1:7
For God hath not given us the spirit of fear; but of power, and of love, and of a sound mind.

F. F. Bosworth understood the importance of overcoming fear and doubt by feeding our faith with the Word of God. Similarly, I once heard an international minister named Keith Moore talk about what a blessing it would be to receive from the Lord what He wanted to give us without fail and without delay. This is what would happen if we could completely eliminate doubt from our daily lives. And this is why it is important for us to starve doubt and feed faith as much as possible by saturating our lives with the Word of God. Faith comes by hearing, and hearing by the Word of God (Romans 10:17).

Moore went on to explain how people begin to believe but circumstances and bad reports shake them. James 1:6-7 reminds us that wavering back and forth can cause failure to receive or delay. In fact, James 1:8 says "A double minded man is unstable in all his ways." Our Lord and Savior Jesus Christ, our perfect example, was completely yielded to the point that doubt was eliminated from his life.

Principle
2

FORGIVENESS IS A MUST

In order to receive healing, it is crucial that you make sure that you are right with God and walking in humility. The first step is to ask Christ to save you if you are not already born again. Even if you are already a Christian, you must examine your heart and confess or acknowledge your sins if you need to be cleansed from any unrighteousness. You must also forgive others of their sins so that you can be in a better place to receive God's mercy. The Scripture clearly teaches that unconfessed sin in your life or having an unforgiving heart can hinder you from being healed.

First Make Sure You Are Saved and Forgiven.

Romans 10:9
That if thou shalt confess with thy mouth the Lord Jesus, and shalt believe in thine heart that God hath raised him from the dead, thou shalt be saved.

Romans 10:13
For whosoever shall call upon the name of the Lord shall be saved.

Isaiah 59:1-2
Behold, the LORD'S hand is not shortened, that it cannot save; neither his ear heavy, that it cannot hear: But your iniquities have separated between you and your God, and your sins have hid his face from you, that he will not hear.

Psalm 66:18
If I regard iniquity in my heart, the Lord will not hear me.

James 5:14-16
Is any sick among you? let him call for the elders of the church; and let them pray over him, anointing him with oil in the name of the Lord: And the prayer of faith *shall save the sick*, and the Lord *shall raise him up*; and if he have committed sins, they shall be *forgiven* him. *Confess your faults* one to another, and pray one for another, that ye may be *healed*. The effectual fervent prayer of a righteous man availeth much.

Notice that the above Scriptures let us know that the Lord *shall* raise the sick up! Not might, not maybe, but *shall*…if we come to the Lord with a *clean heart* and with *faith*. Why would God tell us to pray in such a manner if it was not his will to heal?

Bosworth also explains that *"what water is in the ordinance of Christian baptism, oil is in the ordinance of anointing the sick for healing."* He further points out that even laymen are commanded to confess their faults and pray for one another's healing.

Proverbs 28:13
He that covereth his sins shall not prosper: but whoso confesseth and forsaketh them shall have mercy.

1 John 1:9
If we confess our sins, he is faithful and just to forgive us our sins, and to cleanse us from all unrighteousness.

2 Chronicles 7:14
If my people, which are called by my name, shall humble themselves, and pray, and seek my face, and turn from their wicked ways; then will I hear from heaven, and will forgive their sin, and will *heal* their land.

John 5:8-9, 14
Jesus saith unto him, Rise, take up thy bed, and walk.... And immediately the man was made whole, and took up his bed, and walked.... Afterward Jesus findeth him in the temple, and said unto him, Behold, thou art made whole: sin no more, lest a worse thing come unto thee.

Notice that in the Scripture below, particularly in the last verses listed, Jesus also mentions the need to forgive after he talks about our need to have faith.

Mark 11:23-26
For verily I say unto you, That whosoever shall say unto this mountain, Be thou removed, and be thou cast into the sea; and shall not doubt in his heart, but shall believe that those things which he saith shall come to pass; he shall have whatsoever he saith. Therefore I say unto you, What things soever ye desire, when ye pray, believe that ye receive them, and ye shall have them. And when ye stand praying, forgive, if ye have ought against any: that your Father also which is in heaven may forgive you your trespasses. But if ye do not forgive, neither will your Father which is in heaven forgive your trespasses.

Principle

3

UNDERSTAND GOD'S WILL REGARDING PHYSICAL HEALING

In the New Testament, Jesus never turned anyone away and never lost a case concerning healing. No one was denied healing in the four Gospels or in the book of Acts. He paid the price on the cross to heal all who will come in faith.

Consider the following Scriptures, which demonstrate that Jesus desires to heal all and that he paid the price for the healing of every individual just like he paid the price for everyone's salvation.

Luke 4:40
Now when the sun was setting, all they that had any sick with divers diseases brought them unto him; and he laid his hands on every one of them, and healed them.

Matthew 12:15
But when Jesus knew it, he withdrew himself from thence: and great multitudes followed him, and he healed them all.

Matthew 14:35-36
And when the men of that place had knowledge of him, they sent out into all that country round about, and brought unto him all that were diseased; And besought him that they

might only touch the hem of his garment: and as many as touched were made perfectly whole.

Luke 6:19
And the whole multitude sought to touch him: for there went virtue out of him, and healed them all.

Matthew 8:16-17
When the even was come, they brought unto him many that were possessed with devils: and he cast out the spirits with his word, and healed all that were sick: That it might be fulfilled which was spoken by Esaias the prophet, saying, Himself took our infirmities, and bare our sicknesses.

Acts 10:38
How God anointed Jesus of Nazareth with the Holy Ghost and with power: who went about doing good, and healing *all* that were oppressed of the devil; for God was with him.

Notice that the above Scriptures say that Jesus *healed all who were sick.* Consider the following verse:

John 6:38
For I came down from heaven, not to do mine own will, but the will of him that sent me.

Jesus went about teaching, preaching, and *healing*. If Jesus did the will of the Father by healing *all* who came to him 2,000 years ago, why would he not heal *all* who come with faith in our present time?

In the next Scripture, Christ explains that his believers will be able to ask anything in his name (according to his will) and do even greater works after his exaltation:

John 14:12-14
Verily, verily, I say unto you, He that believeth on me, the works that I do shall he do also; and greater works than these shall he do; because I go unto my Father. And whatso-

ever ye shall ask in my name, that will I do, that the Father may be glorified in the Son. If ye shall ask any thing in my name, I will do it.

Mark 16:15, 17-18
He said unto them, Go ye into all the world, and preach the gospel to every creature.... And these signs shall follow them that believe; In my name shall they cast out devils; they shall speak with new tongues; They shall take up serpents; and if they drink any deadly thing, it shall not hurt them; they shall lay hands on the sick, and they shall recover.

3 John 1:2
Beloved, I wish above all things that thou mayest prosper and be in health, even as thy soul prospereth.

1 Peter 2:24
Who himself bore our sins in His own body on the tree, that we, having died to sins, should live for righteousness—by whose stripes you were healed. (NKJV)

Notice that the last Scripture points out that by Christ's stripes we *were* healed from the sickness of sin—past tense. As it was also pointed out in Matthew 8:16-17, Jesus already paid the price for physical healing, just as he paid it for salvation, but we must receive it by faith. *It is finished!*

If we do not know the will of God and believe that healing is for *all*, we cannot properly claim God's promises to us. We must not just believe that God *can*, but we must know that he *will*.

Consider how Jesus answered the one person in the Bible, a leper, who was not sure of God's willingness to heal:

Matthew 8:2-3
And behold, a leper came and worshiped Him, saying, "Lord, if You are willing, You can make me clean." Then Jesus put out *His* hand and touched him, saying, "I am willing; be cleansed. Immediately his leprosy was cleansed. (NKJV)

The leper did not have the revelation of the Word written clearly in the New Testament like we have it now. Jesus used that leper as an example for all of us so that we could see his willingness to heal. Based on our Old and New Testament scriptural revelations, we no longer have to ask the Lord if he is willing to heal. We must know that he is willing (as long as we meet the conditions of the Word).

Also notice that Mark 9 proves that even though the ministers of Christ (in this case, his disciples) sometime fail to bring forth healing or deliverance because of unbelief, it is still God's will to heal. Notice that Christ healed the epileptic in spite of the unbelief of his disciples, who were divinely commissioned:

Mark 9:23-29
Jesus said unto him, If thou canst believe, all things are possible to him that believeth. And straightway the father of the child cried out, and said with tears, Lord, I believe; help thou mine unbelief. When Jesus saw that the people came running together, he rebuked the foul spirit, saying unto him, Thou dumb and deaf spirit, I charge thee, come out of him, and enter no more into him. And the spirit cried, and rent him sore, and came out of him.... And when he was come into the house, his disciples asked him privately, Why could not we cast him out? And he said unto them, This kind can come forth by nothing, but by prayer and fasting.

Consider the fact that Jesus gave all of his disciples power to heal the sick, and he also commanded them to preach the gospel and heal the sick:

Matthew 10:1
And when he had called unto him his twelve disciples, he gave them power against unclean spirits, to cast them out, and to heal all manner of sickness and all manner of disease.

Matthew 10:8
Heal the sick, cleanse the lepers, raise the dead, cast out devils: freely ye have received, freely give.

Mark 3:14-15
And he ordained twelve, that they should be with him, and that he might send them forth to preach, And to have power to heal sicknesses, and to cast out devils.

Luke 9:2
And he sent them to preach the kingdom of God, and to heal the sick.

Luke 10:9
And heal the sick that are therein, and say unto them, The kingdom of God is come nigh unto you.

Even the Old Testament lets us know about God's ability and desire to heal all sickness and disease:

Psalm 103:2-3
Bless the LORD, O my soul, and forget not all his benefits: Who forgiveth all thine iniquities; who healeth all thy diseases.

Numbers 21:8
And the LORD said unto Moses, Make thee a fiery serpent, and set it upon a pole: and it shall come to pass, that every one that is bitten, when he looketh upon it, shall live.

Psalm 105:37
He brought them forth also with silver and gold: and there was not one feeble person among their tribes.

Jeremiah 17:14
Heal me, O LORD, and I shall be healed; save me, and I shall be saved: for thou *art* my praise.

Jeremiah 30:17
For I will restore health unto thee, and I will heal thee of thy wounds, saith the LORD...

Principle

4

UNDERSTAND THAT JESUS REDEEMED US FROM OUR DISEASES WHEN HE ATONED FOR OUR SINS

Even the Old Testament tells us that one of God's seven redemptive names was Jehovah Rapha (translated as "the Lord your Physician" or "the Lord that heals")

Exodus 15:26
...for I am the LORD that healeth thee.

Galatians 3:13
Christ hath redeemed us from the curse of the law, being made a curse for us: for it is written, Cursed is every one that hangeth on a tree.

The curse included every disease known to man, so there is no disease that God cannot cure. In the same manner that God forgives sins through the atonement of Christ, he also heals diseases through the atonement:

Isaiah 53:4-5
Surely he hath borne our griefs [sicknesses], and carried our sorrows [pains]: yet we did esteem him stricken, smitten of God, and afflicted. But he was wounded for our transgressions, he was bruised for our iniquities: the chastisement of our peace was upon him; and with his stripes we are healed.

Also note that in the original text the words *griefs* and *sorrows* are more accurately translated as "sicknesses" and "pains." The actual Hebrew words are *choli*, "sicknesses," and *makob*, "pains."

Matthew 8:16-17 actually refers to Isaiah 53:4 and gives an accurate translation in reference to Christ's atonement for our physical healing:

Matthew 8:16-17
...and healed all that were sick: That it might be fulfilled which was spoken by Esaias the prophet, saying, Himself took our infirmities, and bare our sicknesses.

The abovementioned New Testament Scripture provides further proof that our Lord and Savior Jesus Christ paid the price for physical healing from sickness and disease as well as deliverance from sin. Christ healed all who came in faith because of the atonement, and he is still healing all who come in faith.

Just as Jesus paid the price for sin on Calvary, he also paid the price for sickness. But we must receive our physical healing by faith, just as we receive eternal salvation of the soul by faith.

We must understand that sin and disease are the works of the devil:

Acts 10:38
How God anointed Jesus of Nazareth with the Holy Ghost and with power: who went about doing good, and healing all that were oppressed of the devil; for God was with him.

Luke 13:16
And ought not this woman, being a daughter of Abraham, whom Satan hath bound, lo, these eighteen years, be loosed from this bond on the sabbath day?

1 John 3:8
For this purpose the Son of God was manifested, that he might destroy the works of the devil.

Luke 10:19
"Behold, I give you the authority to trample on serpents and scorpions, and over all the power of the enemy, and nothing shall by any means hurt you." (NKJV)

Mark 6:56
And whithersoever he entered, into villages, or cities, or country, they laid the sick in the streets, and besought him that they might touch if it were but the border of his garment: and as many as touched him were made whole.

We must also consider the very meaning of the word *salvation*, which many Christians only equate with the saving of the soul. *Soteria* is the Greek word for "salvation," and it relates to deliverance, healing, health, preservation, and soundness. *Sozo* is the Greek word for "saved," and it means to be made whole or healed.

As Dr. R.A. Torrey said many years ago in his book *Divine Healing*, "Individual believers, whether elders or not, have the privilege and the duty to 'pray one for another' in case of sickness, with the expectation that God will hear and heal."

Principle
5

A REVELATION OF MERCY

Psalm 52:8
I trust in the mercy of God forever and ever.

In order to truly get the victory, you must get rid of all doubt concerning God's will regarding physical healing. You must know that it is his will to heal you because he is a merciful and compassionate God. You must be convinced that he is not just able *but is also* willing *to heal you. Many Christians understand that God is powerful enough and able to heal them, but many miss the point that he is willing to heal because of his mercy. As F. F. Bosworth pointed out, we sometimes mistakenly exalt God's power above his mercy.*

Note that in the Scriptures mercy and compassion mean the same thing, so wherever you see the word *compassion* in most of our modern-day translations, it means the same thing as mercy.

God is love, and his love, mercy, and compassion are his greatest motivators for healing and delivering his creation. F. F. Bosworth explained that once individuals caught this simple truth, it opened the floodgates for many more healings to take place. To be full of mercy and compassion means that God has a burning desire, eagerness, or yearning to heal and deliver his people.

Bosworth further explains that:

> *Modern theology magnifies the* power *of God more than it magnifies his* compassion.... *But the Bible reverses this and magnifies His willingness to use his power more than it does the power itself.*

For this reason the Bible says that *God is love*, not that *God is power*. The Bible admonishes us to trust not just in God's power but also in his love and mercy:

Psalm 52:8 says, **"I trust in the mercy of God forever and ever."** Every Christian seems to understand that the Lord is able, but fewer seem to understand that he is also willing because **"the LORD is gracious, and full of compassion [mercy]" (Psalm 145:8).** We must change our focus from saying that he is able to saying that he is merciful and he is willing.

But even beyond knowing that God is willing, we must get a full revelation that **"He delights in mercy" (Micah 7:18 NKJV).**

Asking for God's mercy can reverse the curse! Deuteronomy lets us know that God's mercy is greater than the curse caused by our sins from the past:

Deuteronomy 5:9-10
Thou shalt not bow down thyself unto them, nor serve them: for I the LORD thy God am a jealous God, visiting the iniquity of the fathers upon the children unto the third and fourth generation of them that hate me, And shewing mercy unto thousands of them that love me and keep my commandments.

Deuteronomy 7:9
Know therefore that the LORD thy God, he is God, the faithful God, which keepeth covenant and mercy with them that

love him and keep his commandments to a thousand generations.

God is full of mercy because he is full of love. Once you get a revelation of God's mercy and God's love, it will even drive out your fears:

1 John 4:18-19
There is no fear in love; but perfect love casts out fear, because fear involves torment. But he who fears has not been made perfect in love. We love Him because He first loved us. (NKJV)

More Scriptures of Mercy

Hebrews 4:14-16
Seeing then that we have a great High Priest who has passed through the heavens, Jesus the Son of God, let us hold fast *our* confession. For we do not have a High Priest who cannot sympathize with our weaknesses, but was in all *points* tempted as we are, yet without sin. Let us therefore come boldly to the throne of grace, that we may obtain mercy and find grace to help in time of need. (NKJV)

Psalm 145:8-9
The LORD is gracious, and full of compassion; slow to anger, and of great mercy. The LORD is good to all: and his tender mercies are over all his works.

Psalm 25:1-3, 7, 16-21
Unto thee, O LORD, do I lift up my soul. O my God, I trust in thee: *let me not be ashamed*, let not mine enemies triumph over me. Yea, let none that wait on thee be ashamed: let them be ashamed which transgress without cause.... Remember not the sins of my youth, nor my transgressions: according to thy *mercy* remember thou me for thy goodness'

sake, O LORD.... Turn thee unto me, and have *mercy* upon me; for I am desolate and afflicted. The troubles of my heart are enlarged: O bring thou me out of my distresses. Look upon mine affliction and my pain; and forgive all my sins. Consider mine enemies; for they are many; and they hate me with cruel hatred. O keep my soul, and deliver me: let me not be ashamed; for I put my trust in thee. Let integrity and uprightness preserve me; for I wait on thee.

Psalm 32:10
Many sorrows shall be to the wicked: but he that trusteth in the LORD, *mercy* shall compass him about.

Psalm 86:5-7, 13, 15-17
For thou, Lord, art good, and ready to *forgive*; and *plenteous in mercy* unto all them that call upon thee. Give ear, O LORD, unto my prayer; and attend to the voice of my supplications. In the day of my trouble I will call upon thee: for thou wilt answer me.... For *great is thy mercy* toward me: and thou hast delivered my soul from the lowest hell.... But thou, O Lord, art a God full of compassion, and gracious, longsuffering, and *plenteous in mercy* and truth. O turn unto me, and have *mercy* upon me; give thy strength unto thy servant, and save the son of thine handmaid. Shew me a token for good; that they which hate me may see it, and be ashamed: because thou, LORD, hast helped me, and comforted me.

Psalm 118:1-9
O give thanks unto the LORD; for he is good: because his *mercy endureth for ever*. Let Israel now say, that his mercy endureth for ever. Let the house of Aaron now say, that his mercy endureth for ever. Let them now that fear the LORD say, that his mercy endureth for ever. *I called upon the LORD in distress: the Lord answered me*, and set me in a large place. The LORD is on my side; I will not fear: *what can man do unto [for] me?* The LORD taketh my part with them that help me:

therefore shall I see my desire upon them that hate me. *It is better to trust in the LORD than to put confidence in man.* It is better to trust in the LORD than to put confidence in princes.

Psalm 103:10-13

He hath not dealt with us after our sins; nor rewarded us according to our iniquities. For as the heaven is high above the earth, so *great is his mercy toward them that fear him.* As far as the east is from the west, so far hath he removed our transgressions from us. Like as a father pitieth his children, so the LORD pitieth them that fear him.

Micah 7:18-19

Who is a God like unto thee, that pardoneth iniquity, and passeth by the transgression of the remnant of his heritage? he retaineth not his anger for ever, because *he delighteth in mercy.* He will turn again, he will have *compassion* upon us; he will subdue our iniquities; and thou wilt cast all their sins into the depths of the sea.

Scriptural Examples of God's Mercy

Jonah, a prophet to the nation of Israel, didn't want the assignment to preach to the Ninevites that God gave him. In Jonah 1:2 the Lord told him, **"Arise, go to Nineveh, that great city, and cry against it; for their wickedness is come up before me."** Because these people had plundered, tortured, and killed his fellow Israelites, Jonah felt that the Lord should have punished and destroyed them instead of warning them. Jonah ran away from his responsibility to warn the Ninevites because he was concerned that they might repent and become bene-factors of God's great mercy. When Jonah finally obeyed the Lord and warned the city, the Ninevites repented of their sins, and God showed them great mercy, forgave them, and held back his judgment. **"And God saw their works, that they turned from their evil way; and God repented of the evil, that he had said that he would do unto them; and he did it not (Jonah 3:10).**

Because Jonah wanted to see the Ninevites pay for their gross sins, he got extremely angry, and in his complaint to the Lord he explained that he had never wanted to preach to the Ninevites in the first place because he feared that they would receive mercy from a compassionate God:

Jonah 4:1-2
But it displeased Jonah exceedingly, and he was very angry. And he prayed unto the LORD, and said, I pray thee, O LORD, was not this my saying, when I was yet in my country? Therefore I fled before unto Tarshish: for I knew that thou art a gracious God, and merciful, slow to anger, and of great kindness, and repentest thee of the evil.

The story of the Ninevites is another example of the tremendous magnitude of God's mercy even to the most wicked of all people who are willing to repent and ask the Lord for mercy.

Also consider the fact that even a wicked king like Ahab received mercy and escaped some of God's judgment because he humbled himself:

1 Kings 21:25-29
But there was none like unto Ahab, which did sell himself to work wickedness in the sight of the LORD, whom Jezebel his wife stirred up. And he did very abominably in following idols, according to all things as did the Amorites, whom the LORD cast out before the children of Israel. And it came to pass, when Ahab heard those words, that he rent his clothes, and put sackcloth upon his flesh, and fasted, and lay in sackcloth, and went softly. And the word of the LORD came to Elijah the Tishbite, saying, Seest thou how Ahab humbleth himself before me? because he humbleth himself before me, I will not bring the evil in his days: but in his son's days will I bring the evil upon his house.

And consider the fact that Hezekiah, a righteous king, was spared from death because a merciful God saw his faith and tears:

Isaiah 38:1-5
In those days was Hezekiah sick unto death. And Isaiah the prophet the son of Amoz came unto him, and said unto him, Thus saith the LORD, Set thine house in order: for thou shalt die, and not live. Then Hezekiah turned his face toward the wall, and prayed unto the LORD, And said, Remember now, O LORD, I beseech thee, how I have walked before thee in truth and with a perfect heart, and have done that which is good in thy sight. And Hezekiah wept sore. Then came the word of the LORD to Isaiah, saying, Go, and say to Hezekiah, Thus saith the LORD, the God of David thy father, I have heard thy prayer, *I have seen thy tears*: behold, I will add unto thy days fifteen years.

As Christians we should be careful not to get to the point where we think that healing only comes because of our own righteousness or faith in the power of God. Some Christians also wrongly believe that mercy is only for the sinner. As Christians, we must be cautious not to miss our blessing due to a self-righteousness that causes us to feel that we do not need mercy.

Note that Paul the apostle credited the healing of a fellow believer to the mercy of God:

Philippians 2:27
For indeed he was sick almost unto death; but God had mercy on him, and not only on him but on me also, lest I should have sorrow upon sorrow. (NKJV)

As F. F. Bosworth pointed out, *"In our day most people think of mercy as applied only to the sinner, not knowing that His mercy is also extended to the sick."*

Consider what Jesus said regarding this issue of mercy and self-righteousness when he dealt with the self-righteous religious leaders of his day:

Luke 18:9-14
And he spake this parable unto certain which trusted in themselves that they were righteous, and despised others: Two men went up into the temple to pray; the one a Pharisee, and the other a publican. The Pharisee stood and prayed thus with himself, God, I thank thee, that I am not as other men are, extortioners, unjust, adulterers, or even as this publican. I fast twice in the week, I give tithes of all that I possess. And the publican, standing afar off, would not lift up so much as his eyes unto heaven, but smote upon his breast, saying, God be merciful to me a sinner. I tell you, this man went down to his house justified rather than the other: for every one that exalteth himself shall be abased; and he that humbleth himself shall be exalted.

If You Sow Mercy You Shall Reap Mercy

Notice that Job was healed when he showed mercy and prayed for his friends:

Job 42:10, 12
And the LORD turned the *captivity* of Job, when he *prayed* for his friends: also the LORD gave Job *twice as much* as he had before. So the LORD *blessed the latter end* of Job more than his beginning.

Matthew 5:7
Blessed are the *merciful*: for they shall obtain *mercy*.

The Scriptures also indicate that mistreating people or lacking compassion and respect for others can be a reason for hindered prayers.

1 Peter 3:7
Husbands, likewise, dwell with them with understanding, giving honor to the wife, as to the weaker vessel, and as being heirs together of the grace of life, that your prayers may not be hindered. (NKJV)

Proverbs 21:13
Whoever shuts his ears to the cry of the poor
Will also cry himself and not be heard. (NKJV)

In other words, when you treat people in general with kindness and compassion, you open up bigger doors for the Lord to have greater mercy in your life.

Psalm 41:1-4
Blessed is he who considers the poor; The LORD will deliver him in time of trouble. The LORD will preserve him and keep him alive, And he will be blessed on the earth; You will not deliver him to the will of his enemies. The LORD will strengthen him on his bed of illness; You will sustain him on his sickbed. I said, "Lord, be merciful to me; Heal my soul, for I have sinned against you." (NKJV)

Proverbs 19:17
He who has pity on the poor lends to the Lord,
And He will pay back what he has given. (NKJV)

Judgment and Mercy

As Christians we must also be careful not to judge other Christians who are not healed for one reason or another. Being harsh, judgmental, and overly critical of other Christians who failed to receive healing could cause us not to receive God's mercy when it is needed. The Bible says that we should **"weep with them that weep" (Romans 12:15).** If a Christian dies from sickness, we should show compassion and "weep with them that weep." Even Jesus wept when he heard that Lazarus had died (see John 11:35).

I actually know of Christians who say things like, "If you would have had more faith, your husband would not have died." This is harsh and insensitive. Furthermore, unless God actually gives us a revelation as to why a Christian might have died tragically or prematurely from sickness, we cannot possibly know all of the facts. We are not the judge, but God is. Whenever it is appropriate to do so, we should instruct and encourage people to trust God for healing. But it is not our place to condemn others who might have perspectives about divine healing that are different from ours.

James 2:13
For judgment is without mercy to the one who has shown no mercy. Mercy triumphs over judgment. (NKJV)

Luke 6:36-37
Be ye therefore merciful, as your Father also is merciful. Judge not, and ye shall not be judged: condemn not, and ye shall not be condemned: forgive, and ye shall be forgiven.

The Scripture above does not imply that Christians should never exercise judgment of any kind. First Corinthians 6:3 says, "Know ye not that we shall judge angels? how much more things that pertain to this life?" (see also 1 Corinthians 5:11-13). "Judge not" implies that we should not condemn or make judgment based on incomplete or prejudiced information or based on our own standards (as opposed to the standard of God's Word). Consequently, when led by the Spirit at an appropriate time, a Christian can exercise proper biblical judgment to lovingly correct another believer about what the Bible actually teaches about God's will to heal.

From a Christian perspective we must realize that, even if a precious saint dies tragically or prematurely, if that person was truly saved, then death is not the worst thing that could happen. In other words, a person who dies young with Christ is far better off than a person who lives to be old and dies without Christ. God's perspective on death is not the same as the perspective of unregenerated man. For the Scripture declares the following:

2 Corinthians 5:8
We are confident, I say, and willing rather to be absent from the body, and to be present with the Lord.

Psalm 116:15
Precious in the sight of the LORD is the death of his saints.

1 Thessalonians 4:13-14
But I would not have you to be ignorant, brethren, concerning them which are asleep [in death], that ye sorrow not, even as others which have no hope. For if we believe that Jesus died and rose again, even so them also which sleep in Jesus will God bring with him.

Philippians 1:21-24 (NKJV)
For to me, to live is Christ, and to die is gain. But if I live on in the flesh, this will mean fruit from my labor; yet what I shall choose I cannot tell. For I am hard-pressed between the two, having a desire to depart and to be with Christ, which is far better. Nevertheless to remain in the flesh is more needful for you.

Mercy and Compassion Motivated Christ to Heal

Matthew 14:14
And Jesus went forth, and saw a great multitude, and was moved with compassion toward them, and he healed their sick.

Matthew 20:30-34
And, behold, two blind men sitting by the way side, when they heard that Jesus passed by, cried out, saying, Have mercy on us, O Lord, thou Son of David. And the multitude rebuked them, because they should hold their peace: but they cried the more, saying, Have mercy on us, O Lord, thou Son of David. And Jesus stood still, and called them, and said, What will ye that I shall do unto you? They say unto him, Lord, that our eyes may be opened. So Jesus had compassion on them, and touched their eyes: and immediately their eyes received sight, and they followed him.

Matthew 9:27-29
And when Jesus departed thence, two blind men followed him, crying, and saying, Thou Son of David, have mercy on

us. And when he was come into the house, the blind men came to him: and Jesus saith unto them, Believe ye that I am able to do this? They said unto him, Yea, Lord. Then touched he their eyes, saying, According to your faith be it unto you. And their eyes were opened; and Jesus straitly charged them, saying, See that no man know it.

Mark 10:47-52
And when he heard that it was Jesus of Nazareth, he began to cry out, and say, Jesus, thou Son of David, have mercy on me. And many charged him that he should hold his peace: but he cried the more a great deal, Thou Son of David, have mercy on me. And Jesus stood still, and commanded him to be called. And they call the blind man, saying unto him, Be of good comfort, rise; he calleth thee. And he, casting away his garment, rose, and came to Jesus. And Jesus answered and said unto him, What wilt thou that I should do unto thee? The blind man said unto him, Lord, that I might receive my sight. And Jesus said unto him, Go thy way; thy faith hath made thee whole. And immediately he received his sight, and followed Jesus in the way.

David, a man after God's own heart who had committed adultery, was spared from a greater judgment because he pleaded for mercy in Psalm 51:

Psalm 51:1-3
Have *mercy* upon me, O God, according to thy lovingkind-ness: according unto *the multitude of thy tender mercies* blot out my transgressions. Wash me thoroughly from mine iniq-uity, and cleanse me from my sin. For I acknowledge my transgressions: and my sin is ever before me.

Psalm 103 further demonstrates that David understood God's mercy regarding the physical healing of diseases and spiritual healing from sin:

Psalm 103:2-4, 8-14
Bless the LORD, O my soul, and forget not all his benefits: Who forgiveth all thine iniquities; who healeth all thy diseases; Who redeemeth thy life from destruction; who crowneth thee with *lovingkindness and tender mercies*.... The Lord is *merciful and gracious*, slow to anger, and *plenteous in mercy*. He will not always chide: neither will he keep his anger for ever. He hath not dealt with us after our sins; nor rewarded us according to our iniquities. For as the heaven is high above the earth, so *great is his mercy* toward them that fear him. As far as the east is from the west, so far hath he removed our transgressions from us. Like as a father *pitieth his children*, so the LORD pitieth them that fear him. For he knoweth our frame; *he remembereth that we are dust*.

Proverbs 28:13
He that *covereth his sins* shall not prosper: but whoso confesseth and forsaketh them shall have *mercy*.

Psalm 130:3-4
If You, Lord, should keep account *and* treat [us according to our] sins, O Lord, who could stand? [Ps. 143:2; Rom. 3:20; Gal. 2:16] But there is forgiveness with You, [just what man needs] that You may be reverently feared *and* worshiped. [Deut. 10:12] (AMPLIFIED)

Closing Remarks Regarding Mercy

We are all products of God's mercy! Even if we have faith to be healed, it is because of his mercy and grace that we have a mind with which to have faith. It is also because of his mercy and grace that he sent a book, a Bible, or a preacher to teach us faith: **"So then faith cometh by hearing, and hearing by the word of God" (Romans 10:17).**

Psalm 23:6
Surely goodness and mercy shall follow me all the days of my life: and I will dwell in the house of the LORD forever.

Principle

6

YOU MUST BELIEVE IT BEFORE YOU SEE IT

According to the Scriptures (see Mark 11:23-24), we must believe that our prayer for healing is heard before we see the full manifestation of the answer to our prayer. In other words, we must not focus on symptoms of sickness but on the promises in God's Word regarding healing. Through faith and patience, we can inherit the promise of God (see Hebrews 6:12).

Mark 11:23-24
For verily I say unto you, That whosoever shall say unto this mountain, Be thou removed, and be thou cast into the sea; and shall not doubt in his heart, but shall believe that those things which he saith shall come to pass; he shall have whatsoever he saith. Therefore I say unto you, What things soever ye desire, when ye pray, believe that ye receive them, and ye shall have them.

Understand the Difference Between Mere Hope and Real Faith

Understand that faith is not just hoping for or expecting a change in the future, but *faith is now*. It is accepting God's Word now as a done deal before you actually see the full manifestation of the blessing. *It is finished!*

If we truly believe that something is a done deal, then we will thank God for it even before we fully see it with the natural eye—the same way we would thank a credible friend or family member if that person promised to buy us a car next week. We would act as though we had the car and make plans on how we were going to use the car even before picking it up, simply because we believed that the person's word was good. Because God's Word is better than the word of any person, we should continually praise him for healing even before we fully see the physical manifestation of it. Our faith should cause us to believe that God has already heard—*past tense*—our prayers as Jesus taught in Mark 11:24.

It is critical for us to understand this concept in order to be fully assured of our healing. You must get out of the future tense, which is mere hope, and get into the past tense, which is believing that what you have asked for is already done by faith. You must know the difference between mere hope and real faith. *Faith grabs a hold of God's promise now.*

F. F. Bosworth said,

> *God always heals when He can get the right cooperation.... Continue to believe that God gave you what you asked for when you prayed, thanking and praising Him for what He has given, and it will always materialize.*

Always meditate on God's word and trust in it. Jesus overcame the devil's lies by saying, **"It is written,"** and we must do the same. The greatest weapon we have is the Word of God. As F. F. Bosworth stated,

> *You have exactly the same reason for expecting to be healed that you had for expecting to be saved.... The consecrated Christian will not consciously tolerate sin for a moment, and yet how tolerant some are towards sickness. They will even pet and indulge their aches and pains instead of resisting them as the words of the devil.*

Don't focus on the symptoms, but focus on the promise. The symptom might be the pain from arthritis or a cancerous growth on the neck like Cheryl Lehmann had. But, by faith, we must believe God for our healing even if the symptoms don't leave right away. Even if there is no improvement after prayer, the sick must believe God for healing when everything they see seems contrary to God's promise to heal.

Even Abraham continued to trust in God by bringing Isaac to the altar. This was a test that Abraham passed because Abraham didn't focus on the circumstances. Faith focuses only on the Word of God, not on circumstances, feelings, or symptoms. **"For we walk by faith, not by sight" (2 Corinthians 5:7).** Bosworth said that if we are encouraged by what we see (an improvement in our condition for instance) more than we are encouraged by the Word of God alone, then God might allow our symptoms of sickness to come back to test our faith. Faith is about *the Word of God* and nothing else!

We must say and believe only what God says, and our actions must line up with God's promises. In other words, we must believe it before we see it. In John 20:29, Jesus said to doubting Thomas, **"Thomas, because thou hast seen me, thou hast believed: blessed are they that have not seen, and yet have believed."** God tested Abraham's faith by commanding Abraham to offer Isaac up as a sacrifice when Abraham knew that God's promise to him could not be fulfilled without Isaac. The lesson is that the Lord wants us to walk by faith, not by sight or circumstance. Consequently, the Lord will sometimes test our faith in order to strengthen it, not to weaken us.

As Bosworth taught, our faith must be persistent, unwavering and steadfast:

> *We are to think faith, speak faith, act faith, and keep it until the promise is fulfilled. By being occupied with symptoms or feelings, we violate the conditions and thereby turn off the switch of His power.*

James 1:6-8
But let him ask in faith, nothing wavering. For he that wavereth is like a wave of the sea driven with the wind and

tossed. For let not that man think that he shall receive any thing of the Lord. A double minded man is unstable in all his ways.

We must expect God's promises to come to pass when we pray and act on faith before we see the full manifestation of the healing. We must have an expectation or unshakable confidence that is greater than mere hope alone. **"Now faith is the substance of things hoped for, the evidence of things not seen" (Hebrews 11:1). Also, "we walk by faith, not by sight" (2 Corinthians 5:7).** By faith we must know that by his stripes we are healed in spite of the symptoms of sickness that we might see. Because of faith, we thank God for the healing even before we see the full manifestation of it, and we can also begin testifying to others that by his stripes we are healed. This is a way of acting on faith.

Notice how Jesus spoke when he had the faith to raise Lazarus from the dead. While Lazarus was still dead, Jesus said, **"Father, I thank You that You have heard Me" (John 11:41 NKJV).** Faith does not wait to see results before it will testify or believe God. Just as Jesus thanked God the Father in advance, we should do the same, saying, "Lord I thank you that you have heard my prayers"—not "Lord, if it be your will, please heal me."

In Mark 11:24, Jesus said that we must consider our prayers answered before we actually see the answer:

Mark 11:24
Therefore I say unto you, What things soever ye desire, when ye pray, believe that ye receive them, and ye shall have them.

1 John 5:14-15
And this is the confidence that we have in him, that, if we ask any thing according to his will, he heareth us: And if we know that he hear us, whatsoever we ask, we know that we have the petitions that we desired of him.

It is also important to understand that symptoms do not always go away instantly and healing is not always instant. Some were healed as they went. **"And it came to pass, that, as they went, they were cleansed" (Luke 17:14).** The better we understand how to apply the Word and act on the Word, the sooner we can see the full manifestation of the healing that we are asking for.

In the same manner, the sooner a sinner understands what the Word says about salvation, the sooner he or she can be saved. Why is it that some people hear the gospel and are saved right away, while others take years to finally be saved after first hearing the message of salvation, and some are never saved at all? It is simply because some receive and apply the words of salvation right away while others don't. The same is often the case in reference to applying the Word of God in order to be healed.

Below are some additional Scriptures that relate to praying and believing according to the will of God:

1 John 3:22
And whatsoever we ask, we receive of him, because we keep his commandments, and do those things that are pleasing in his sight.

John 14:12-14
Verily, verily, I say unto you, He that believeth on me, the works that I do shall he do also; and greater works than these shall he do; because I go unto my Father. And whatsoever ye shall ask in my name, that will I do, that the Father may be glorified in the Son. If ye shall ask any thing in my name, I will do it.

John 15:7
If ye abide in me, and my words abide in you, ye shall ask what ye will, and it shall be done unto you.

John 16:23-24
And in that day ye shall ask me nothing. Verily, verily, I say unto you, Whatsoever ye shall ask the Father in my name, he

will give it you. Hitherto have ye asked nothing in my name: ask, and ye shall receive, that your joy may be full.

Matthew 21:21-22
If ye have faith, and doubt not ... all things, whatsoever ye shall ask in prayer, believing, ye shall receive.

Hebrews 6:12
That ye be not slothful, but followers of them who through faith and patience inherit the promises.

Consider what Jesus said about asking and receiving as it relates to the goodness of God the Father:

Matthew 7:7-12
Ask, and it shall be given you; seek, and ye shall find; knock, and it shall be opened unto you: For every one that asketh receiveth; and he that seeketh findeth; and to him that knocketh it shall be opened; Or what man is there of you, whom if his son ask bread, will he give him a stone? Or if he ask a fish, will he give him a serpent? If ye then, being evil, know how to give good gifts unto your children, how much more shall your Father which is in heaven give good thing to them that ask him? Therefore all things whatsoever ye would that men should do to you, do ye even so to them: for this is the law of the prophets.

Principle

7

UNDERSTAND THE POWER OF THE MOUTH

1 Peter 2:24
Who his own self bare our sins in his own body on the tree, that we, being dead to sins, should live unto righteousness: by whose stripes ye were healed.

Belief and Confession

Confession is simply believing and saying the same thing that God says about us or about our condition. It is the act of making our words agree with the Word of God. If God says that something is one way, then we should not say something contrary with our lips.

As previously mentioned, Isaiah 53:4-5 states that Christ paid the price for our physical sicknesses as well as our sins. Matthew 8:16-17 further reminds us of this: **"and he cast out the spirits with *his* word, and healed all that were sick: That it might be fulfilled which was spoken by Esaias the prophet, saying, Himself took our infirmities, and bare our sicknesses."**

According to 1 Peter 2:24, Christ has already—past tense—paid the price and redeemed us from our diseases when He atoned for our sins, so we can confess that "I am healed [not shall be healed] by his stripes."

Confession, of course, does not imply that we should go off the deep end and deny things that God never told us to deny. F. F. Bosworth stated the following:

Of course we are not to say to others that our healing is fully manifested before it is. God does not say that. But you can say to those who ask you, "I am standing on the Word of God."

If you have cancer in your body, you are lying if you say, "I don't have any cancer." But you are telling the truth if you say, "With His stripes I am healed according to Isaiah 53:5 or 1 Peter 2:24, and I am just waiting for God to manifest the healing by removing this cancer." In other words, we should not deny what exists, but we should call for what we desire according to God's promises. Romans 4:17 lets us know that God calls things that are not manifest as though they were manifest.

Romans 4:17
(As it is written, I have made thee a father of many nations,) before him whom he believed, *even* God, who quickeneth the dead, and calleth those things which be not as though they were.

Our thoughts and words should never focus on our failures, inadequacies, or doubts, and Bosworth even points out that confessing a lack of faith or confessing fear increases doubt and can also let Satan in. *"We will never rise above our confession,"* he declares. We must realize that just as faith comes by what we hear (Romans 10:17) and confess (Romans 10:9-10), doubt also comes by what we hear and confess.

Since words are powerful and "death and life are in the power of the tongue" (Proverbs 18:21), we must be careful what we say on a daily basis. We should not be in the habit of saying things like, "I hate you," or "You Dummy," even jokingly. Concerning our finances, we should not say things like, "I'll always be broke and I'll never get out of debt." In Mark 11:23 Jesus said *we shall have what we say*, and this principle works in the negative as well as in the positive. Also, we should not be in the habit of saying things like, "my tooth ache is killing me." Instead we should confess God's word as long as it takes until we get the results God promises. Don't focus on the fact that you are tired, sick, and weak, but say things like, "In the name of Jesus I am getting stronger," according to Joel 3:10 which says "Let the weak say, I am strong." Also say, "With his stripes I am healed" according to

1 Peter 2:24 and Isaiah 53:5. Rather than saying something like, "I just can't sleep at night," before you get ready to go to bed you can say, "Thank you Lord for helping me to sleep and rest properly tonight."

On the other side of the coin, it should be noted that saying something negative (Example: "I'm losing my mind.") doesn't necessarily mean it's going to happen, just like saying something positive (Example: "I'm going to become debt-free.") doesn't necessarily mean it is going to happen. This is because you are what you believe, not just what you say. You have to truly believe something before it will work for you—either positively or negatively. The main point that I am trying to make here is that Christians at times can be careless with their words and what they say. Obviously if you keep saying something, no matter how ridiculous it may sound at first, if you keep saying it, you are more likely to believe it, and if you are believing it and saying it, and it is something negative, then the law of sowing and reaping kicks in.

Confession is a continual activity, and it is something that should be done out loud with the mouth. It is a proven fact that when you say something out loud with your mouth, the words you speak will have a greater impact on your inner heart and mind. This is why the Bible even tells us that the way to salvation is to confess with the mouth and believe in the heart that God has raised Christ from the dead (Romans 10:9-10). What we confess out loud with the mouth is a powerful thing. Therefore, we should confess daily the things we are dealing with, saying and agreeing with what the Word says in order to renew the mind. We should also realize that developing faith is a process and we should simply start right where we are, even using our faith to overcome smaller problems. Avoid the extreme of trying to become a "faith giant" overnight which could lead to the type of foolishness or presumption that could cause you to hurt yourself.

For example, it would be foolish to destroy your glasses in order to try to prove that you have faith to see clearly without them. If you destroy your glasses and God has not given you a full manifestation of restored vision, you will probably crash while driving to work! So don't be foolish. Also, it might not be wise for you to stop using your medication if you have not built your faith up to a certain point. Furthermore, there is nothing wrong with using doctors and medication in certain situations. I once heard a very practical preacher say that medicine plus faith equals a greater ability to be healed because you are combining the best of the natural with the supernatural—and taking medicine is not necessarily a sign that you lack faith. Faith and confession are powerful elements, but we must remember to apply God's principles with proper balance.

Not understanding that faith must be exercised and that faith has different levels can cause a person to become confused, judgmental, condemned or puffed up. Thoughts like, "Since I don't have faith like him, I'm nothing as a Christian" can bring self-condemnation. On the other hand, prideful statements like, "If everybody else had strong faith like me, they could be healed right away," or, "If his faith was strong enough, then he would not have been sick so long," can lead to a judgmental spirit or a lack of compassion toward others who are struggling with sickness. Just like the human body will grow stronger and more muscular the more we lift weights or exercise the body, our faith will also grow stronger the more we feed it with the Word of God and the more we exercise it by stepping out and believing God for supernatural things. Just as an individual who just started an exercise program will not become a perfect physical specimen overnight, we must also understand that individuals who are new at exercising their faith will also go through a growing process. Some individuals are simply at higher levels of faith than others because they have been taught the Word longer and have also exercised their faith more than others. Consequently, rather than being so quick to judge others, we should be more concerned about encouraging others to grow in faith by hearing, speaking, and applying the Word of God more.

Consider what the Bible says regarding the power of the mouth and mind:

Proverbs 18:21
Death and life are in the power of the tongue.

Proverbs 6:2
Thou art snared with the words of thy mouth, thou art taken with the words of thy mouth.

Joel 3:10
Let the weak say, I am strong.

Proverbs 23:7
For as he thinketh in his heart, so is he.

Mark 11:23
[Jesus said,] "For verily I say unto you, That whosoever shall say unto this mountain, Be thou removed, and be thou cast into the sea; and shall not doubt in his heart, but shall believe that those things which he saith shall come to pass; he shall have whatsoever he saith."

Saying the right thing is important. But, as alluded to earlier, believing is also important. We must also avoid the trap of confessing our faith with our lips and doubting with our hearts. The mind and the lips must work together in concert. Bosworth made the statement that our confession rules us. Therefore, we must continually confess the Word, and the Word will heal us. I have often made the statement that we are all products of what we say, hear, think, and see. This can be backed up with the following Scriptures as well as with those that were already mentioned:

Romans 10:17
So then faith cometh by hearing, and hearing by the word of God.

Philippians 4:8
Finally, brethren, whatsoever things are true, whatsoever things are honest, whatsoever things are just, whatsoever things are pure, whatsoever things are lovely, whatsoever things are of good report; if there be any virtue, and if there be any praise, think on these things.

Most importantly, we must confess Christ our Lord and Savior and make him Lord of our lives. After we are right with God spiritually, we will then be in the place to be fully assured of our physical healing. By saying, **"The LORD is my shepherd; I shall not want" (Psalm 23:1)**, you are also making your confession for your other natural needs as well. Never underestimate the power of your confession.

Avoid Faith-Destroying Words

According to Bosworth, Christians should not use "faith-destroying words" like "if it be your will" when praying to God for healing, because the Bible already reveals God's will regarding his desire to heal. Saying this is similar to saying, "Lord, if it is your will, save my soul so that I do not have to go to hell." In terms of receiving salvation of the soul, we must know that it is God's will to save the soul (just as we must know it is his will to heal the body). As previously stated, confession and believing play a role in healing, just as in salvation we must confess with our mouths and believe in our hearts:

Romans 10:9-10
That if thou shalt confess with thy mouth the Lord Jesus, and shalt believe in thine heart that God hath raised him from the dead, thou shalt be saved. For with the heart man believeth unto righteousness; and with the mouth confession is made unto salvation.

There are times when it is very noble and correct to pray things like, "Lord, if it is your will, I pray that you will bless me to get a job in such-and-such company." But when God has revealed his will in his Word regarding a particular matter, praying, "If it is your will" can be a sign of doubt and unbelief.

2 Peter 3:9
The Lord is not slack concerning *His* promise, as some count slackness, but is longsuffering toward us, not willing that any should perish but that all should come to repentance. (NKJV)

The above Scripture allows us to know that, just because some people will never be saved, we should not think that God has failed or that it was not his will to save them. To put it bluntly, God does not want anyone to go to hell. But God will let you go to hell if you refuse to believe his words of eternal life. The same is true of physical healing. Even though some wonderful Christian people have died tragically or prematurely of sickness or disease, this does not mean that it was not God's will to heal them. Rather than put all the responsibility on the Lord every time a Christian is not healed, why not consider the fact that in some cases even Christians do not appropriate their faith by believing and confessing their healing based on God's promises.

Hebrews 11:6
But without faith it is impossible to please him: for he that cometh to God must believe that he is, and that he is a rewarder of them that diligently seek him.

God's Word is His will. The more you speak God's Word with your mouth over and over again, the more it will kindle your faith. Also, the more you say God's Word, the more God watches over it in order to perform it or accomplish his purposes.

Jeremiah 1:12 (NAS)
Then the LORD said to me, You have seen well, for I am watching over my word to perform it.

Isaiah 55:11
So shall my word be that goeth forth out of my mouth: it shall not return unto me void, but it shall accomplish that which I please, and it shall prosper _in the thing_ whereto I sent it.

Lay Hands on the Sick and Speak to the Problem

Mark 11:23-24
For verily I say unto you, That whosoever shall say unto this mountain, Be thou removed, and be thou cast into the sea; and shall not doubt in his heart, but shall believe that those things which he saith shall come to pass; he shall have whatsoever he saith. Therefore I say unto you, What things soever ye desire, when ye pray, believe that ye receive them, and ye shall have them.

Notice in the Scripture above Jesus mentions the ability a child of God has to speak to the mountain. Since the mountain can represent a disease such as cancer, God has given us power to lay hands on the sick and to command cancer to leave a body by the power of our mouths: "I command cancer to come out of this body in the name of Jesus," is the type of prayer that can be prayed with scriptural authority. There are scriptural examples when Jesus or his disciples simply spoke to the condition and brought healing. There are other examples in which Christ or his disciples brought deliverance by laying on of hands along with speaking to the sickness simultaneously. These are scriptural principles that any believing Christian can practice to bring healing and deliverance by the leading of the Spirit.

The Scriptures below demonstrate the biblical principle of laying on hands and speaking the Word in order to bring forth healing and deliverance. As I once heard a preacher declare, "Don't just speak to God about your problem; speak to your problem!"

Matthew 8:2-3
And, behold, there came a leper and worshipped him, saying, Lord, if thou wilt, thou canst make me clean. And Jesus put forth *his* hand, and touched him, saying, I will; be thou clean. And immediately his leprosy was cleansed.

Matthew 9:27-30
And when Jesus departed thence, two blind men followed him, crying, and saying, *Thou* Son of David, have mercy on us. And when he was come into the house, the blind men came to him: and Jesus saith unto them, Believe ye that I am able to do this? They said unto him, Yea, Lord. Then touched he their eyes, saying, According to your faith be it unto you. And their eyes were opened...

Mark 9:25-26
When Jesus saw that the people came running together, he rebuked the foul spirit, saying unto him, Thou dumb and deaf spirit, I charge thee, come out of him, and enter no more into him. And *the spirit* cried, and rent him sore, and came out of him...

Mark 16:17-18
And these signs shall follow them that believe; In my name shall they cast out devils; they shall speak with new tongues; They shall take up serpents; and if they drink any deadly thing, it shall not hurt them; they shall lay hands on the sick, and they shall recover.

Acts 3:6-8
Then Peter said, Silver and gold have I none; but such as I have give I thee: In the name of Jesus Christ of Nazareth rise up and walk. And he took him by the right hand, and lifted *him* up: and immediately his feet and ankle bones received strength. And he leaping up stood, and walked, and entered with them into the temple, walking, and leaping, and praising God.

Acts 14:8-10
And there sat a certain man at Lystra, impotent in his feet, being a cripple from his mother's womb, who never had walked: The same heard Paul speak: who stedfastly beholding him, and perceiving that he had faith to be healed, Said with a loud voice, Stand upright on thy feet. And he leaped and walked.

Acts 16:16,18
And it came to pass, as we went to prayer, a certain damsel possessed with a spirit of divination met us, which brought her masters much gain by soothsaying...And this did she many days. But Paul, being grieved, turned and said to the spirit, I command thee in the name of Jesus Christ to come out of her. And he came out the same hour.

Acts 28:8
And it came to pass, that the father of Publius lay sick of a fever and of a bloody flux: to whom Paul entered in, and prayed, and laid his hands on him, and healed him.

Principle

8

THE SACRIFICE
OF PRAISE

In spite of symptoms of illness, don't forsake the sacrifice of praise on a continual basis. When someone has already provided a gift for you, you thank that person. Once you claim your healing, you no longer have to ask God to heal you over and over again. You can simply thank him for the healing continually as a sign of your faith and your gratitude, despite any symptoms you might have. This is your way of letting the Lord know that you are not wishy-washy and that you have accepted the healing that he paid for with his death on the cross.

James 1:6-8
But let him ask in faith, nothing wavering. For he that wavereth is like a wave of the sea driven with the wind and tossed. For let not that man think that he shall receive any thing of the Lord. A double minded man is unstable in all his ways.

Hebrews 13:15
By him therefore let us offer the sacrifice of praise to God continually, that is, the fruit of our lips giving thanks to his name.

Psalm 22:3
But thou art holy, O thou that inhabitest the praises of Israel.

Isaiah 61:3
To appoint unto them that mourn in Zion, to give unto them beauty for ashes, the oil of joy for mourning, the garment of praise for the spirit of heaviness...

Psalm 107:20-21
He sent his word, and healed them, and delivered them from their destructions. Oh that men would praise the LORD for his goodness, and for his wonderful works to the children of men!

Because **"faith without works is dead" (James 2:20),** praising God in advance, even before you see the full manifestation of your healing, is one of your greatest weapons. Notice that even Jesus thanked God the Father in advance before Lazarus was raised from the dead when he said, **"Father, I thank You that You have heard Me" (John 11:41** NKJV**).**

Psalm 34:1
I will bless the LORD at all times: his praise shall continually be in my mouth.

John 9:31 (NKJV)
Now we know that God does not hear sinners; but if anyone is a worshiper of God and does His will, He hears him.

1 Thessalonians 5:18
In every thing give thanks: for this is the will of God in Christ Jesus concerning you.

Praising God, even in trials, is a demonstration of faith (as opposed to doubt) and gratitude (as opposed to ungratefulness). It is a demonstration of faith in action.

When you praise the Lord continually, it is your way of letting the Lord know that you refuse to waver like a double-minded man and that you will believe his Word with an attitude of gratitude in spite of your circumstances. *It is the sacrifice of praise that will help to shut the door on the devil's works.*

Principle
9

UNDERSTAND GOD'S CONDITIONAL PROMISES

Obedience Is the Key

Some theologians teach that it is God's will for some Christians to stay sick for God's glory. If this is true, then it would be correct to say that Jesus robbed God the Father of his glory at times because Jesus healed all who came to him! Therefore, we know that God does not get glory by allowing his children to stay sick. Nothing in the Bible teaches us this.

Examining Ourselves

It should be pointed out that some Christians are defeated by sickness and disease or die prematurely because of disobedience or failure to properly discern the Lord's body. If we acknowledge our sin and turn from our waywardness, God's Word shows us that the Lord can then have mercy upon us and deliver us. The following verses in 1 Corinthians bring out the point that the failure to properly discern the Lord's body can actually cause premature death (see the appendix for more on this topic).

1 Corinthians 11:28-32
But let a man examine himself, and so let him eat of *that* bread, and drink of *that* cup. For he that eateth and drinketh unworthily, eateth and drinketh damnation to himself, not discerning the Lord's body. For this cause many *are* weak and sickly among you, and many sleep [die]. For if we would judge ourselves, we should not be judged. But when we are judged, we are chastened of the Lord, that we should not be condemned with the world.

Meeting the Conditions of God's Promises

There are many promises in God's Word that are conditional while some are not. If we do not obey the Lord, then we can open up the door for calamity, as the following verse notes.

Isaiah 1:19-20
If ye be willing and obedient, ye shall eat the good of the land: But if ye refuse and rebel, ye shall be devoured with the sword: for the mouth of the LORD hath spoken it.

Psalm 25:10
All the paths of the LORD are *mercy* and truth unto such as keep his covenant and his testimonies.

2 Chronicles 7:14
If my people, which are called by my name, shall humble themselves, and pray, and seek my face, and turn from their wicked ways; then will I hear from heaven, and will forgive their sin, and will *heal* their land.

Obedience

The Word of God also implies that sickness and disease can sometimes be connected to specific sins or disobedience in our lives, just as our healing can come because of our obedience to God's laws.

Exodus 15:26
And said, If thou wilt diligently hearken to the voice of the LORD thy God, and wilt do that which is right in his sight, and wilt give ear to his commandments, and keep all his statutes, I will put none of these diseases upon thee, which I have brought upon the Egyptians: for I am the LORD that healeth thee.

The Bible also lets us know that before we can properly resist the devil, who desires to see us destroyed by sickness, we must first submit to God:

James 4:7
Submit yourselves therefore to God. Resist the devil, and he will flee from you.

Romans 12:1
I beseech you therefore, brethren, by the mercies of God, that ye present your bodies a living sacrifice, holy, acceptable unto God, which is your reasonable service.

Notice that Naaman the leper was totally obedient to God's instructions by washing in the Jordan seven times before he was healed (see 2 Kings 5:10-14).

Psalm 84:11
No good thing will he withhold from them that walk uprightly.

Deuteronomy 7:9
Know therefore that the LORD thy God, he is God, the faithful God, which keepeth covenant and mercy with them that love him and keep his commandments to a thousand generations.

In closing, it is important to realize that Jesus will not force us to receive physical healing, just like he will not force anyone to receive salvation of the soul. Obviously our sovereign God can decide to heal any person at random without the person making any prayers or petitions for healing. But there is something we must typically do in order to receive the blessing of physical healing, and we must engage the will in order to be made whole. Notice how Jesus asked the man at the pool of Bethesda, **"Do you want to be made well?" (John 5:6 NKJV).** Jesus knew He was able to make the man whole, but the Lord wanted to engage the man's will in the matter. To further engage the man's will and to put faith in action, Jesus commanded him, **"Rise, take up your bed, and walk" (John 5:8).** Then the Scripture says, **"immediately the man was made well, took up his bed, and walked" (John 5:9).**

(Also see Principle 6 for more Scripture references regarding God's conditional promises.)

Principle
10

THE POWER OF UNIFIED PRAYER

We must not forsake the important role that unified prayer in the church plays in terms of bringing forth a greater anointing for healing.

Acts 4:29-31
And now, Lord, behold their threatenings: and grant unto thy servants, that with all boldness they may speak thy word, By stretching forth thine hand to heal; and that signs and wonders may be done by the name of thy holy child Jesus. And when they had prayed, the place was shaken where they were assembled together; and they were all filled with the Holy Ghost, and they spake the word of God with boldness.

Acts 5:12-16
And by the hands of the apostles were many signs and wonders wrought among the people; (and they were all with one accord in Solomon's porch. And of the rest durst no man join himself to them: but the people magnified them. And believers were the more added to the Lord, multitudes both of men and women.) Insomuch that they brought forth the sick into the streets, and laid them on beds and couches, that at the least the shadow of Peter passing by might overshadow some of them. There came also a multitude out of the cities round about unto Jerusalem, bringing sick folks, and

them which were vexed with unclean spirits: and they were healed *every one.*

Because the church was on one accord regarding the issue of healing for the sick, miraculous healings took place. F. F. Bosworth said:

> *They prayed "the prayer of faith" before the sick were brought into the streets of Jerusalem. It was not the faith of a single evangelist, but the faith of an entire company of believers. This brought healing to everyone in the streets of Jerusalem after Christ's ascension.... It was not the faith of a lone or solitary evangelist but that of a Spirit-filled church.... A Spirit-filled and praying church produces an atmosphere in which it is easy for God to work. This makes it difficult for the devil to interfere.*

Listed below are more verses that illustrate the benefits of unity among God's people. When we become more unified in prayer, faith, and works, we achieve greater results together than one person can achieve independently:

Leviticus 26:8
And five of you shall chase an hundred, and an hundred of you shall put ten thousand to flight: and your enemies shall fall before you by the sword.

Matthew 18:18-20
Verily I say unto you, Whatsoever ye shall bind on earth shall be bound in heaven: and whatsoever ye shall loose on earth shall be loosed in heaven. Again I say unto you, That if two of you shall agree on earth as touching any thing that they shall ask, it shall be done for them of my Father which is in heaven. For where two or three are gathered together in my name, there am I in the midst of them.

Also see Ecclesiastes 4:9-12 (two are better than one) and James 5:14 (call for the elders of the church).

APPENDIX

ALL BELIEVERS CAN PRAY FOR THE SICK

What Jesus Commanded His Disciples

Matthew 10:7-8
And as ye go, preach, saying, The kingdom of heaven is at hand. Heal the sick, cleanse the lepers, raise the dead, cast out devils: freely ye have received, freely give.

Elders and Even Laymen Are Commanded to Pray for the Healing of the Sick

James 5:14-17
Is any sick among you? let him call for the elders of the church; and let them pray over him, anointing him with oil in the name of the Lord: And the prayer of faith shall save the sick, and the Lord shall raise him up; and if he have committed sins, they shall be forgiven him. Confess your faults one to another, and pray one for another, that ye may be healed. The effectual fervent prayer of a righteous man availeth much. Elias was a man subject to like passions as we are, and he prayed earnestly that it might not rain: and it rained not on the earth by the space of three years and six months

Mark 16:17-18
And these signs shall follow them that believe; In my name shall they cast out devils; they shall speak with new tongues; They shall take up serpents; and if they drink any deadly thing, it shall not hurt them; they shall lay hands on the sick, and they shall recover.

GOD'S SEVEN REDEMPTIVE NAMES

The names listed here reveal what our redemption includes and cover all human needs in the atonement.

1. JEHOVAH-SHAMMAH means "the Lord is present."

2. JEHOVAH-SHALOM means "the Lord is our Peace."

3. JEHOVAH-RA-AH means "the Lord is my Shepherd."

4. JEHOVAH-JIREH means "the Lord will provide."

5. JEHOVAH-NISSI means "the Lord our Banner."

6. JEHOVAH-TSIDKENU means "the Lord our Righteousness."

7. JEHOVAH-RAPHA means "I am the Lord that healeth thee" or "I am the Lord thy Physician."

EXAMPLES OF LONG LIFE FROM GOD'S WORD

Understand that God wants you to live out your days with good health.

Psalm 91:15-16
He shall call upon me, and I will answer him: I will be with him in trouble; I will deliver him, and honour him. With long life will I satisfy him, and shew him my salvation.

Exodus 23:25-26
And ye shall serve the LORD your God, and he shall bless thy bread, and thy water; and I will take sickness away from the midst of thee. There shall nothing cast their young, nor be barren, in thy land: the number of thy days I will fulfil.

Ecclesiastes 7:17
Do not be overly wicked, Nor be foolish: Why should you die before your time? (NKJV)

Psalm 118:17
I shall not die, but live, and declare the works of the Lord.

Deuteronomy 34:7
Moses was one hundred and twenty years old when he died. His eyes were not dim nor his natural vigor diminished. (NKJV)

Joshua 14:10-11
...and now, here I am this day, eighty-five years old. As yet I am as strong this day as on the day that Moses sent me; just as my strength was then, so now is my strength for war, both for going out and for coming in. (NKJV)

(Joshua 24:29 says Joshua was one hundred and ten years old when he died.)

THE POWER OF UNBELIEF

For we say that faith was reckoned to Abraham for righteousness (Romans 4:9).

F. F. Bosworth, in his book *Christ the Healer*, spoke very strongly against unbelief. If we are accounted righteous by believing God, then "it is unbelief that constitutes us unrighteous," according to Bosworth. Some of his statements were as follows:

> *Unbelief is wicked and unrighteous because it hinders and sets aside the Divine program which consists of all that God has promised to do in response to faith. No wonder that it was the sin of unbelief of which God sent the Spirit to convict the world. Anything short of our having a living faith for the will and work of God to be done, even though we may call it religion, is something else in the place of His righteousness, and therefore it is unrighteous.*

Jesus himself addressed the unbelief issue in Matthew 17, identifying it as the primary reason that his disciples were unable to cast the devil out of a man's epileptic son.

Matthew 17:16-18
And I brought him to thy disciples, and they could not cure him. Then Jesus answered and said, O faithless and perverse generation, how long shall I be with you? how long shall I suffer you? bring him hither to me. And Jesus rebuked the devil; and he departed out of him: and the child was cured from that very hour.

Since faith is the key that unlocks the door, if necessary, ask God to help you to overcome doubt or unbelief. God gives grace to the humble, so he will help you if you ask. This is evident in Mark 9:24, where the man with the sick child cried out with tears, "Lord, I believe; help thou mine unbelief." The Holy Spirit, your Helper, will grant you the ability to overcome doubt and unbelief if you *totally depend* on Him and *focus* on God's Word.

2 Corinthians 12:9
"My grace is sufficient for thee: for my strength is made perfect in weakness."

1 John 4:4
Ye are of God, little children, and have overcome them: because greater is he that is in you, than he that is in the world.

Romans 8:37
Nay, in all these things we are more than conquerors through him that loved us.

Do You Need More Faith or Less Doubt?

Author and international Bible teacher Andrew Wommack is a man of great faith who says that "Most people have been taught how to disbelieve." His daily *Gospel Truth* radio and television broadcasts reach millions of people worldwide. On occasions when individuals in distress have personally told him about their incurable diseases, it is not uncommon for Andrew to respond by proclaiming something like, "This is a small thing for God to handle."

On his June 10, 2014, *Gospel Truth* television broadcast, Andrew testified that he has seen thousands of people healed of incurable diseases. He has prayed for thousands of sick people who have received supernatural healing as a result of the prayer of faith, and the Charis Bible College founder reminds us that the Word of God should be more real to us than medication or doctors. Because most of us hear so much about sicknesses or the medications or procedures designed to fight diseases, many people focus only on these natural things, according to Andrew. It is unfortunate, he explains, that many of these same individuals are filled with doubt and unbelief when it comes to the things of God. It is hard for some people to believe that by His stripes we are healed, even though the Bible teaches this.

Andrew further explains that some doctors will spread hopelessness and unbelief by telling their chronically ill patients that they only have so many months to live, while neglecting to encourage their patients to look to God for hope or supernatural help that is greater than what any doctor can give. Consequently, many patients are robbed of the knowledge that would help them to trust in God to supernaturally heal them of a disease that is naturally incurable.

In spite of the culture of unbelief that surrounds us, this has not stopped Andrew from praying the prayer of faith and witnessing supernatural miracles for numerous souls. Making it very clear that he is not at all against the medical profession, Andrew points out that medicine has even saved the lives of many Christians. The point he wants to bring out, however, is that the medical profession only consists of natural, inferior, limited human ability, whereas faith in God provides limitless opportunities for individuals to get supernatural help that doctors cannot provide.

With the well-meaning intent to fight a life-threatening illness, patients who are diagnosed with incurable diseases are sometimes consumed with learning as much as possible about the disease itself. Since such a consumption of negative information can increase doubt and unbelief, Andrew encourages people to study what the Bible teaches about healing rather than focus on the facts about the destructive disease. In other words, it is more beneficial to focus on things that build faith rather than focusing on negative things that foster unbelief.

Andrew explains that it is unbelief—not so much the lack of faith—that even causes some Bible-believing Christians to lose the battle to the oppressive forces of sickness and disease. A small amount of "mustard seed" faith is all you need, he says. If you do not eventually see the visible results you would like to see regarding your healing, it is not necessarily because you don't have enough faith, but it is likely because you have unbelief. This is why it is very important to focus on the Word of God and shut out negative influences and contrary voices when you need a miraculous healing from God. "Your little mustard seed amount of faith would be more than enough to receive whatever miracle you need from God if you did not have all of that unbelief that negated it—that wiped it out," says Andrew.

To further prove this point, Andrew references Scriptures like Matthew 17:14-21, where Jesus told his disciples that they could not cure the epileptic because of their unbelief. Andrew explains that Jesus' disciples had the mustard seed faith that they needed, but their faith was of no effect in this particular instance because of their doubt and unbelief. In other words, the disciples prayed the prayer of faith, but they focused too much on the outburst of epilepsy or the physical manifestation of the child being tormented by the demonic force. They allowed the negative circumstances or the symptoms that they witnessed with their natural eyes to cause them to doubt. Consequently, the Lord told His disciples that they could overcome this type of doubt and unbelief by disciplining themselves through prayer and fasting.

At first glance, it is easy to assume that Jesus is making the point that this type of powerful demonic sickness can only be overcome through prayer and fasting. However, Andrew teaches that if you look at this Scripture in context, Jesus is actually making the point that this kind of *unbelief* is overcome by prayer and fasting. In this same passage of Scripture, Jesus also told his disciples that only mustard seed faith is needed to move mountains, making the point that their problem was not a lack of faith; their problem was actually the doubt or unbelief that they allowed to cancel out their faith. In essence, he was telling his disciples that they needed a higher level of spiritual discipline to overcome the doubt or unbelief that caused them to lack the ability to bring forth the deliverance that was needed. Could it be that more Christians would drive out unbelief and see many more miracles if more of us disciplined our lives through the power of prayer and fasting as Jesus suggested?

On the June 10, 2014, *Gospel Truth* television broadcast, Andrew Wommack also shared the story of how he once received a grossly misguided medical diagnosis when he went to a doctor to get a physical. After Andrew took a treadmill test, which consisted of jogging with electrodes attached to his chest, the doctor looked at the results of the test on paper and told Andrew that he was in big trouble: "You have a serious heart problem, and you might need to have open heart surgery before this day is over."

Since Andrew knew he was in good health and did not believe he had a heart condition, he refused to just blindly take the doctor's word. Looking sternly at the medical professional, Andrew dared to say, "That's a lie. I don't have any heart problem. You look at that paper and tell me that I have a heart condition!"

Startled by Andrew's bold challenge, the doctor started backing down from his original statement: "It could be nothing, but you were just a little bit abnormal and you ought to get it checked out."

Andrew further challenged the doctor, saying: "That's not what you said in the first place. You claimed that I had a heart condition and might need surgery before the day is out!"

Andrew says he then rebuked this doctor and condemned the words that the doctor spoke over him until the doctor tore up the paper in frustration and told him, "You're fine. Leave. Get out of here!"

Andrew says, "I would never let a doctor come in and pronounce death over me and let it go unchecked." Shortly after the incident with the doctor, the international Bible teacher took another test from another physician that totally verified that his heart was fine with no problem whatsoever. While sharing his second opinion, the doctor also instructed Andrew to never rely on those treadmill tests, since they are apparently wrong about fifty percent of the time.

The point of this story is obviously not to discredit all doctors, because sometimes doctors are correct when they diagnose their patients. The point is to simply remind us that we must be careful not to put too much confidence in man's word. We must put all of our hope and trust in the Word of God, because Christ is our ultimate healer.

REASONS WHY SOME DON'T GET HEALED

A Lack of Knowledge and a Lack of Teaching

Insufficient instruction is the first thing that Bosworth cites as the reason that some fail to receive healing. "Faith cometh by hearing" (Romans 10:17). A lack of knowledge and a lack of teaching lead to a lack of steadfast faith.

James 1:6-8 says that our faith should not waver. Because of a lack of knowledge and instruction regarding God's will concerning healing, many church members today are not praying on one accord like they did in the early church. Bosworth made a critical statement about this in the form of a question:

> *Since we are members one of another, may not the blame for the failure of some to receive healing today be largely due to the unbelieving part of the church itself?*

As pointed out in the Introduction, there are some who attempt to theologically justify man's failure to be healed as God's failure to heal. And there are others who will allow misguided theology to prevent them from obeying the biblical command to pray the prayer of faith that will save the sick (see James 5:14-15).

Bosworth boldly declared,

> *I, for one, will preach all the Gospel if I never see another man saved or healed as long as I live. I am determined to base my doctrines on the immutable word of God, not on phenomena or human experience.*

The Unbelief of an Entire Church or Region

Mark 6:5-6
And he could there do no mighty work, save that he laid his

hands upon a few sick folk, and healed them. And he marvelled because of their unbelief.

If Jesus, the perfect Son of God, was hindered from doing mighty works because of community unbelief, then it should not be difficult to understand how some individuals during our present day fail to receive miracles. The fact that Jesus himself was hindered because of the unbelief of others further proves that doubt, unbelief, and the traditions of men are still hindering many from being healed or receiving miracles today. Upon examining the Scriptures thoroughly, we discover that faith and enlightenment make a tremendous difference as to whether or not one receives healing from the Lord. Jesus said, "If thou canst believe, all things are possible to him that believeth" (Mark 9:23).

Failure to Build up Faith by Studying the Word

The late Kenneth E. Hagin, international Bible teacher and Rhema Bible Training College founder, was strongly influenced by F. F. Bosworth, and Hagin constantly referred to Bosworth's teachings on divine healing.

In his book entitled *Praying To Get Results*, Hagin shared a very compelling yet sad story of a case in which his sister lost a battle to cancer because she neglected to build up her faith through the Word: *"Years ago, I learned that my sister had cancer. I went to the Lord in prayer on her behalf. I battled with the devil for her life. The Lord told me she would live and not die. The cancer was curtailed, and she had no more symptoms. Five years passed, and then she developed an entirely different form of cancer in another part of her body. There was no relation to the first cancer; it was a different type.*

"My sister went down in weight to only 79 pounds. The Lord kept telling me that she was going to die. I kept asking the Lord why I couldn't change the outcome. He told me she had had five years in which she could have studied the Word and built up her faith (she was saved), but she hadn't done it. He told me that she was going to die, and she did. This is a sad example, but it's so true."

Luke 12:48 teaches us that to whom much is given, much is required. Because the sister of this great man of faith didn't take advantage of the opportunity God gave her to build up her own faith, she lost the battle.

The Need to Cast Out an Evil Spirit

Matthew 8:16-17
When the even was come, they brought unto him many that were possessed with devils: and he cast out the spirits with his word, and healed all that were sick: That it might be fulfilled which was spoken by Esaias the prophet, saying, Himself took our infirmities, and bare our sicknesses.

Matthew 10:1
And when he had called unto him his twelve disciples, he gave them power against unclean spirits, to cast them out, and to heal all manner of sickness and all manner of disease.

Mark 9:25
When Jesus saw that the people came running together, he rebuked the foul spirit, saying unto him, Thou dumb and deaf spirit, I charge thee, come out of him, and enter no more into him.

As the above Scriptures imply, there are times when an affliction is caused by an evil spirit that must be cast out. In addition to casting out deaf and dumb spirits, Jesus also cast out the epileptic spirit. F. F. Bosworth pointed out that it was not uncommon for his ministry team to see people instantly delivered when they rebuked the afflicting spirit by speaking in the authority of Christ's name.

Thorn in the Flesh Theology

The erroneous "thorn in the flesh" theology, which implies that remaining sick glorifies God, is another reason that many have not received healing. This theology is supported by the belief that Paul's thorn in the flesh was a physical disease or sickness but has no real scriptural basis. Bosworth asserts that this unscriptural premise has sent thousands of sufferers to premature graves and kept multitudes of others from receiving healing. *Christ the Healer* by F. F. Bosworth devotes an entire chapter to this topic and does an excellent job in explaining from a biblical standpoint that Paul's thorn in the flesh was a person and not a sickness or a disease. Bosworth also explains that the expression "thorn in the flesh" is not in one single instance used in the Bible to represent sickness but always refers to people or personalities. And Paul also referred to his thorn in the flesh as "the messenger of Satan" (the Greek word for "messenger," *angelos*, always refers to a person, not a thing). Furthermore, in the book of Corinthians, when the Apostle Paul stated that his "thorn in the flesh" was "the messenger of Satan to buffet me" (2 Corinthians 12:7), he mentioned a long list of troubles as his buffeting, but disease is not mentioned once. Bosworth further points out that in the book of Numbers Moses referred to the inhabitants of Canaan (people, not things) as thorns in the side:

Numbers 33:55
But if ye will not drive out the inhabitants of the land from before you; then it shall come to pass, that those which ye let remain of them shall be pricks in your eyes, and thorns in your sides, and shall vex you in the land wherein ye dwell.

Breaking Natural Laws

Breaking natural laws is another reason that some fail to be healed. Bosworth said, "Let it be remembered that the natural laws are God's laws and that they are as divine as are His miracles."

Due to a lack of knowledge concerning the natural laws related to health and nutrition, some individuals damage their bodies by eating the wrong foods or by overeating. Some of these same individuals will constantly come to the Lord over and over again to be healed of self-inflicted sickness that is caused by abusing their bodies with very poor nutritional habits or even through substance abuse. Best-selling books like *The Maker's Diet* have reminded the Christian church that much of our sickness and disease or lack of ability to receive healing is often linked to poor nutritional habits. These habits can often be corrected so that the body can be restored to greater health through natural means. Furthermore, God can still show us mercy by healing us miraculously even if we have abused our bodies by breaking certain health laws. But we should not test God by continuing to violate his natural or spiritual laws.

Pride or Lack of Humility

I was very blessed to hear an excellent teaching by a prominent pastor that inspired me to deal with the issue of humility as it relates to healing.

Although making a confession is important, it is not all there is to being healed. In fact, confession without true honesty and humility can hinder one's ability to be healed or delivered. For example, it is not honest or correct to pretend that you are strong in a certain area when you are actually weak. This type of pretense actually leads to denial of the truth. It is honest and true, however, to confess that through the Lord's strength you have victory and grace to overcome your weakness, although you are helpless and weak without him. This is based on the Scriptures that say, "I can do all things through Christ who strengthens me" (Philippians 4:13 NKJV) and "without Me [Christ] you can do nothing" (John 15:5 NKJV). The Scripture does admonish us to be strong and to even confess that we are strong at times (Joshua 1:6 and Joel 3:10). But the Scriptures never tell us to boast in or rely on our own strength, or to pretend that we are strong in and of ourselves when we are actually weak. The Scripture tells us to "be strong in the Lord, and in the power of His might" (Ephesians 6:10 NKJV). Even the Apostle Paul said, "And He [Christ] said to me, 'My grace is sufficient for you, for My strength is made perfect in weakness.' Therefore most gladly I will rather boast in my infirmities, that the power of Christ may rest upon me. Therefore I take pleasure in infirmities, in reproaches, in needs, in persecutions, in distresses, for Christ's sake. For when I am weak, then I am strong" (2 Corinthians 12: 9-10 NKJV). Like the Apostle Paul, we must be balanced enough to admit that without Christ we are weak, but with Christ we are strong.

You are actually living a lie if you deny your sin and confess to others that you are strong and victorious, while you are actually being defeated by an addiction or sinful habit on a regular basis. This type of false confession is not faith. It is denial and it is pride. You first need to honestly confess your "negative" sin to God (Proverbs 28:13, 1 John 1:9, James 5:14-16) before you can make an honest "positive" confession about being free from sin by the power of God. When we are humble enough to admit our sin or our weakness, we can then open up the door to receive God's grace to be healed or delivered. James 4:6-7 (NKJV) says, "God resists the proud, But gives grace to the humble. Therefore submit to God. Resist the devil and he will flee from you." Sometimes good Christian people get tired of resisting. They quit, give up, and die prematurely because of battle fatigue or even due to a lack of humility. I once heard Pastor Keith Moore tell a story about a Christian woman who was not happy because she could not understand why it was taking so long for the Lord to heal a "good Christian woman" like her, while a sinner who did a lot of bad things came to a church service she was at, then got saved and healed instantly. In response to the woman's complaint, the Lord laid a question on Keith Moore's heart: "What does her being a good woman have to do with her being healed?" The bottom line, explained Keith Moore, is that you are not saved or healed by good works. You are saved or healed by grace through faith.

When we approach the Lord with humility, the Lord can then grant us the grace we need to be healed or delivered. But if we approach the Lord in an arrogant way, acting as though it is our own faith, righteousness, or Scriptural knowledge that will save us, God could very well resist us because of our pride. Ultimately, humility and faith must work hand in hand. The humble heart realizes that without the grace of God, it is not even possible to have faith.

2 Chronicles 7:14 says, "If my people, which are called by my name, shall humble themselves, and pray, and seek my face, and turn from their wicked ways; then will I hear from heaven, and will forgive their sin, and will heal their land." This lets us know that in order to be healed, the number one thing we need to do is to humble ourselves. Although having faith to be healed is an important part of the process, humility is even more important—because God resists the proud, but gives grace to the humble. And without the Lord's mercy and grace, we would not even have the steadfast faith to believe God for our healing. Therefore, God's grace comes before and is greater than our faith. Rather than thinking something like, "I can be healed because of my great faith," it is better to know that "by God's grace I can be healed by faith." In other words, don't get proud about the fact that you have faith, because you only have faith because of God's grace. Consequently, it is better to put the emphasis on the role that God's grace and mercy plays in the healing process as opposed to put-

ting too much emphasis on our faith. Like salvation, healing is by grace through faith. Because Jesus paid the price, healing is yours. But you must resist the enemy's lies and you must possess it. What has been provided by grace must be possessed by faith!

Miscellaneous

Other reasons that Bosworth cited for the failure of some to be healed include the unbelief of the praying minister, an unforgiving spirit or the need to seek forgiveness, the seeking of instant miracles rather than healing, neglecting to receive the Holy Spirit (usually not applied to those who are not taught their privilege of being filled with the Spirit according to the book of Acts), the sick person's sin, and a focus on symptoms or improvement more than on God's promises.

BIBLICAL EXAMPLES OF WHY SOME ARE NOT HEALED AND WHY SOME DIE PREMATURELY

Since the references below are Old Testament and New Testament examples, it is important to point out that we now have greater access to grace and mercy for healing through the blood of Christ because we are under the New Covenant which is a better covenant. The point of these examples is not to imply that you should not trust God for healing because of some sin from your past. But the purpose is to remind us that violation of God's principles can sometimes prevent healing from going forth—especially when there is a lack of repentance or a lack of humility in the heart of the individual seeking healing.

Why King David's Child Was Not Healed

In this Old Covenant example, the Scriptures below explain why David's child, who was a direct result of David's adultery with Bathsheba, was not healed in spite of David's prayers.

2 Samuel 12:13-18
And David said unto Nathan, I have sinned against the LORD. And Nathan said unto David, The LORD also hath put away thy sin; thou shalt not die. Howbeit, because by this deed thou hast given great occasion to the enemies of the LORD to blaspheme, the child also that is born unto thee shall surely die. And Nathan departed unto his house. And the LORD struck the child that Uriah's wife bare unto David, and it was very sick. David therefore besought God for the child; and David fasted, and went in, and lay all night upon the earth. And the elders of his house arose, and went to him, to raise him up from the earth: but he would not, neither did he eat bread with them. And it came to pass on the seventh day, that the child died.

Why King Asa Wasn't Healed of a Foot Disease

At one time King Asa trusted in the Lord (see 2 Chronicles 16:7-8), but toward the end of his reign he lived and died in shame because he trusted in man more than God. It is obviously not wrong for a person to seek the assistance of a physician at times. Asa displeased God, however, because he sought the physicians and did not seek God at all.

2 Chronicles 16:7-8
And at that time Hanani the seer came to Asa king of Judah, and said unto him, Because thou hast relied on the king of Syria, and not relied on the LORD thy God, therefore is the host of the king of Syria escaped out of thine hand. Were not the Ethiopians and the Lubims a huge host, with very many chariots and horsemen? yet, because thou didst rely on the LORD, he delivered them into thine hand.

2 Chronicles 16:12-13
And Asa in the thirty and ninth year of his reign was diseased in his feet, until his disease was exceeding great: yet in his disease he sought not to the LORD, but to the physicians. And Asa slept with his fathers, and died in the one and fortieth year of his reign.

Why Gehazi, Elisha's Servant, Got Leprosy

Gehazi's shallow spiritual condition and greed came to the surface and caused him to be struck with a disease when he took silver and other items from Naaman against Elisha's wishes and also lied to the prophet Elisha.

2 Kings 5:25-27
But he went in, and stood before his master. And Elisha said unto him, Whence comest thou, Gehazi? And he said, Thy servant went no whither. And he said unto him, Went not mine heart with thee, when the man turned again from his chariot to meet thee? Is it a time to receive money, and to receive garments, and oliveyards, and vineyards, and sheep, and oxen, and menservants, and maidservants? The leprosy therefore of Naaman shall cleave unto thee, and unto thy seed for ever. And he went out from his presence a leper as white as snow.

Why the Plague Came upon the Israelites

Although Moses was totally submitted to God, was more humble than any man on earth (see Numbers 12:3), and followed the Lord's instructions in leading his people out of bondage, the Israelites still complained. Consequently, the Israelites were judged because they murmured and complained against God and Moses. They were sick and dying because they had been bitten by fiery serpents. Similar to the type of atonement that Christ applied to himself, the Lord instructed that the brazen serpent be lifted up on a pole and looked upon for healing.

Numbers 21:4-9
And they journeyed from mount Hor by the way of the Red sea, to compass the land of Edom: and the soul of the people was much discouraged because of the way. And the people spake against God, and against Moses, Wherefore have ye

brought us up out of Egypt to die in the wilderness? for there is no bread, neither is there any water; and our soul loatheth this light bread. And the LORD sent fiery serpents among the people, and they bit the people; and much people of Israel died. Therefore the people came to Moses, and said, We have sinned, for we have spoken against the LORD, and against thee; pray unto the LORD, that he take away the serpents from us. And Moses prayed for the people. And the LORD said unto Moses, Make thee a fiery serpent, and set it upon a pole: and it shall come to pass, that every one that is bitten, when he looketh upon it, shall live. And Moses made a serpent of brass, and put it upon a pole, and it came to pass, that if a serpent had bitten any man, when he beheld the serpent of brass, he lived.

Why King Jehoram Died of a Disease of the Intestines

2 Chronicles 21 shows that disobedience and defiance of God's laws can cause afflictions to come upon an individual as well as on an entire region.

2 Chronicles 21:12-19

And there came a writing to him from Elijah the prophet, saying, Thus saith the LORD God of David thy father, Because thou hast not walked in the ways of Jehoshaphat thy father, nor in the ways of Asa king of Judah, But hast walked in the way of the kings of Israel, and hast made Judah and the inhabitants of Jerusalem to go a whoring, like to the whoredoms of the house of Ahab, and also hast slain thy brethren of thy father's house, *which were* better than thyself: Behold, with a great plague will the LORD smite thy people, and thy children, and thy wives, and all thy goods: And thou *shalt have* great sickness by disease of thy bowels, until thy bowels fall out by reason of the sickness day by day.

Moreover the LORD stirred up against Jehoram the spirit of the Philistines, and of the Arabians, that *were* near the Ethiopians: And they came up into Judah, and brake into it, and carried away all the substance that was found in the king's house, and his sons also, and his wives; so that there was never a son left him, save Jehoahaz, the youngest of his sons. And after all this the LORD smote him in his bowels with an incurable disease. And it came to pass, that in process of time, after the end of two years, his bowels fell out by reason of his sickness: so he died of sore diseases.

Why Some of the People in the Corinthian Church (New Testament) Died Prematurely

Failure to properly discern the Lord's body can cause individuals to be defeated by sickness or die before their time.

Do you properly discern the Lord's body? Do you understand that it was broken just for you to receive divine physical healing and health? Just as we cannot take it lightly that the blood was shed for the forgiveness of our sins, we must not diminish the purpose of Christ's suffering for our physical healing. Some Christians read these Scriptures in 1 Corinthians 11 and take them lightly—not properly applying this truth or not properly discerning the Lord's body. This sort of ignorance, callousness, or carelessness towards God's sacrifice while taking Holy Communion can lead to unnecessary sickness or even premature death (see 1 Corinthians 11:30). In 1 Corinthians 11:29, when the Apostle Paul told us to discern the Lord's body, he was referring to Christ's suffering for our physical healing. **1 Corinthians 11:24 says, "And when he had given thanks, he brake it, and said, Take, eat: this is my body, which is broken for you: this do in remembrance of me."** Do you realize that the bread you eat when you partake of Holy Communion symbolizes Christ's physical suffering for our physical healing and refers to the body of our Lord Jesus Christ when he bore our sins and sicknesses on the cross? **Isaiah 53:5 says, "But he was wounded for**

our transgressions, he was bruised for our iniquities: the chastisement of our peace was upon him; and with his stripes we are
healed." Likewise, the wine taken in Holy Communion symbolizes
Christ's shed blood for the forgiveness of sins—because "without
shedding of blood is no remission" (Hebrews 9:22). Every time we
partake of Holy Communion, it is important to understand or discern
the truth that the Lord paid the price with his body by suffering on the
cross so we can experience divine healing. Discerning this valuable
truth about the Lord's bodily sacrifice for our physical healing is what
it means to partake of Holy Communion in a worthy manner. As a
result of applying this truth, God's people will not be defeated by
sickness or suffer premature death.

1 Corinthians 11:28-32
**But let a man examine himself, and so let him eat of *that*
bread, and drink of *that* cup. For he that eateth and drinketh
unworthily, eateth and drinketh damnation to himself, not
discerning the Lord's body. For this cause many *are* weak
and sickly among you, and many sleep [die]. For if we would
judge ourselves, we should not be judged. But when we are
judged, we are chastened of the Lord, that we should not be
condemned with the world.**

Why Ananias and Sapphira Died Prematurely

In Acts chapter 5 (another New Testament example), Ananias and his
wife Sapphira both dropped dead at Peter's rebuke because of their
lies and blatant lack of reverence towards God.

Acts 5:3-6
**But Peter said, Ananias, why hath Satan filled thine heart
to lie to the Holy Ghost, and to keep back part of the price
of the land? Whiles it remained, was it not thine own? and
after it was sold, was it not in thine own power? why hast
thou conceived this thing in thine heart? thou hast not lied
unto men, but unto God. And Ananias hearing these words
fell down, and gave up the ghost [died]: and great fear**

came on all them that heard these things. And the young men arose, wound him up, and carried him out, and buried him.

Why the Disciples Could Not Cure the Epileptic

Jesus cited exercising mustard-seed faith, along with overcoming unbelief with greater consecration through prayer and fasting, as a means to bring forth greater healing and deliverance from demonic oppression.

Matthew 17:14-21

And when they were come to the multitude, there came to him a certain man, kneeling down to him, and saying, Lord, have mercy on my son: for he is lunatick [he has epilepsy], and sore vexed: for ofttimes he falleth into the fire, and oft into the water. And I brought him to thy disciples, and they could not cure him. Then Jesus answered and said, O faithless and perverse generation, how long shall I be with you? how long shall I suffer you? bring him hither to me. And Jesus rebuked the devil; and he departed out of him: and the child was cured from that very hour. Then came the disciples to Jesus apart, and said, Why could not we cast him out? And Jesus said unto them, Because of your unbelief: for verily I say unto you, If ye have faith as a grain of mustard seed, ye shall say unto this mountain, Remove hence to yonder place; and it shall remove; and nothing shall be impossible unto you. Howbeit this kind goeth not out but by prayer and fasting.

Also note that according to Isaiah 58:8, fasting benefits us by producing better physical health: **"Your healing shall spring forth speedily..."** (NKJV)

Why Jesus Could Not Do Miracles in His Hometown of Capernaum

Matthew 13:58
And he did not many mighty works there because of their unbelief.

Mark 6:5-6
And he could there do no mighty work, save that he laid his hands upon a few sick folk, and healed them. And he marvelled because of their unbelief.

If Christ himself, the perfect Lamb of God, was limited in the mighty works that he could perform in his hometown of Nazareth because of the community's unbelief, is it unreasonable to believe that there are many in our communities today who fail to receive healing because of their unbelief? In many instances, the Scripture clearly demonstrates that Christ healed individuals according to their faith while others failed to receive miracles due to unbelief.

How Naaman Was Healed of Leprosy

Naaman the leper was totally obedient to God's simple instructions by washing in the Jordan seven times before he was healed. This example in Scripture brings out the point that some are not healed because they don't comply, while others are healed as a result of following the Lord's instructions with humility.

2 Kings 5:10-14
And Elisha sent a messenger unto him, saying, Go and wash in Jordan seven times, and thy flesh shall come again to thee, and thou shalt be clean. But Naaman was wroth, and went away, and said, Behold, I thought, He will surely come out to me, and stand, and call on the name of the LORD his God, and strike his hand over the place, and recover the leper. Are not Abana and Pharpar, rivers of Damascus, better than all

the waters of Israel? may I not wash in them, and be clean? So he turned and went away in a rage. And his servants came near, and spake unto him, and said, My father, if the prophet had bid thee do some great thing, wouldest thou not have done it? how much rather then, when he saith to thee, Wash, and be clean? Then went he down, and dipped himself seven times in Jordan, according to the saying of the man of God: and his flesh came again like unto the flesh of a little child, and he was clean.

How the Blind Man Was Healed at the Pool of Siloam

The blind man followed the instructions of Christ and washed in the pool of Siloam. He believed for his healing before he saw his healing and was healed as he went.

John 9:6-7
When he had thus spoken, he spat on the ground, and made clay of the spittle, and he anointed the eyes of the blind man with the clay, And said unto him, Go, wash in the pool of Siloam, (which is by interpretation, Sent.) He went his way therefore, and washed, and came seeing.

Contemporary Examples

As we can see from the previously mentioned examples, there are many reasons why some are healed and others are not. But we must be careful not to put the responsibility on the Lord when a person is not healed and dies tragically or prematurely.

I am reminded of the story of a well-known, contemporary minister who attempted to help a woman who needed to be healed. The minister, who had seen the Lord heal others through his ministry, prayed the prayer of faith and believed that the Lord would heal the woman. One day the sick woman expressed to the minister that she was ready to go home to be with the Lord because she felt like her life had been "hell on earth." She had gone through all types of problems with relationships and with her children, among other things. She was simply tired of living and felt that heaven was a better place for her to go. The woman died shortly thereafter, and the minister was taught a critical lesson. He learned that he could not override another person's will even if he had the faith for that person's healing.

A similar principle is demonstrated in Matthew 9. Jesus had faith to heal the blind men, but before he healed them he asked them a question: "Believe ye that I am able to do this?" (Matthew 9:28). After they responded, "Yes, Lord," Jesus then touched their eyes, saying, "According to your faith be it unto you. And their eyes were opened" (Matthew 9:29-30). There are some things that the Lord will only do according to the individual's faith or desire, and in the case of the previously mentioned woman and minister, the woman did not have the faith or desire to be healed.

It is important to point out that this does not mean that it was not the Lord's will to heal her. She was simply beaten down and tired of being on this planet.

Famous healing evangelist Jack Coe is an unfortunate example of what can happen if a person continually violates natural health laws. In December of 1956, Coe became critically ill. He simply thought he was suffering from exhaustion, but he was eventually diagnosed with polio. After being admitted to the hospital, he remained unconscious most of the time until he eventually passed away early in 1957 at the age of thirty-eight.

Jack Coe was used by God in a mighty way in the healing ministry. But it was definitely no secret that Coe had abused his body and neglected his health. Unfortunately, he had developed the extreme habits of overworking, overeating, and failing to get proper rest. After his crusades, he would often eat heavy, unhealthy meals at 3:00 a.m. and was extremely overweight as a result. In spite of the fact that he was used as an instrument to heal thousands, Jack Coe simply was not a good steward over his own body, and he paid a great price for it. It was even reported that Coe inwardly possessed the body of a 90-year-old man because of the abuse it suffered.

Though some might want to attribute Coe's death to the will of God, Coe apparently died prematurely because he violated many natural health laws and failed to make efforts to correct his life in this area.

It is a little easier for some to understand why Jack Coe suffered an untimely death based on his consistently poor health habits. But some Christians get confused if an enlightened minister who apparently lived a balanced life dies in a sickly manner that is contrary to the minister's own beliefs concerning divine healing. Although the Lord is able to keep us from faltering until the very end, it is important to point out that even a person of great faith who has lived the most exemplary or honorable life can sometimes fall short at the end of the journey. Moses, a righteous man who was more humble than any man on earth (see Numbers 12:3), in his old age made the critical mistake of disobeying God and in frustration striking a rock against God's instruction. Consequently, the Lord judged Moses and did not permit him to enter into the Promised Land.

Once again, unless the Lord reveals to us why a Christian "misses the Promised Land" or fails to receive healing, it is not our place to judge. The Scriptures show us that Moses was one of God's most obedient servants who simply made a crucial mistake that he had to pay for at the end of his lifetime. As this relates to healing, the point to be made is that even if the most honorable and faithful Christian believer does not see the results that the Bible promises concerning healing, we should not be so quick to put all the responsibility on the Lord. God never fails to deliver what he promises, but sometimes even the best of men fall short in making it to the Promised Land or receiving the promise of God for one reason or another. Although Moses missed the Promised Land, he is still one of the greatest servants of God who ever walked the earth.

FAITH VS. FEELING

F. F. Bosworth mentioned the seeking of miracles rather than healing as one of the reasons that some fail to be healed. Although God does sometimes miraculously heal in an instant, it is important to realize that healing is often a process and is not always instant. In Luke 17:14, the Bible declares that the lepers were healed as they went. Some individuals cast away their confidence and fail to receive their healing because they don't see instant results.

Just as Bosworth pointed out that some aren't healed because they seek instant miracles instead of healing, I would also like to add that, in a similar fashion, some aren't healed because they seek feelings or experiences above the Word of God.

Some of our more expressive churches are wonderful places in which to feel the presence of God while we are worshipping or receiving prayer at the altar. But we must be careful never to base our faith only on what we feel. Since the Scriptures say that God inhabits the praises of his people, vibrant worship and praise in a church service can be an extremely powerful and positive experience. I have discovered that it can be a wonderful thing to have a good feeling while we are in church, to sense or feel the awesome presence of God. And, personally, I would not enjoy attending a church where I never "felt" God moving in the presence of the people.

I also enjoy driving in my car at times and listening to worship music that sometimes causes tears of joy to flow down my face. I am a grown man, and I am not a wimp, but there is something about God's awesome goodness that can make even the hardest of men break down and cry at times. When you truly love something or someone, it is natural to show it with your emotions or your feelings—the same way that men get extremely emotional when the sports team they love or respect is winning a game. The Lord gave us feelings, and he gave them to us for a purpose. But our purpose is not to trust in our feelings more than we trust in the Word.

In some of our local churches, some of the same wonderful saints will go to the altar over and over again to get a touch from the preacher or to get a feeling of being delivered. If we constantly go to the altar for the same problems over and over again just to get a feeling or a sensation, we can begin to put our trust more in our feelings than in the Word of God. In many cases, what these saints will experience is a temporary relief, and they will continue to come back to the altar with the same problems for years.

It is true that God's awesome power can deliver people from sickness or sin at the altar, and he sometimes does it instantly. The Lord also uses some ministers in a mighty fashion as an instrument to deliver people miraculously at church services or crusades. This was also evident in Bosworth's awesome ministry. There were thousands who received miraculous healings at his meetings. But Bosworth himself was also quick to point out that it is important to trust in the Word rather than just seek miracles, because there is a difference between a healing and a miracle.

Though God sometimes performed instant healings in Bosworth's meetings, Bosworth exhorted those who didn't receive instant healings not to cast away their confidence, because healing is often a process. The point to remember is that the minister is simply an instrument in the hands of God, and we must not seek the gift more than the giver. In other words, we must not seek the one who lays hands more than we seek the Word of the Lord. When an individual seeks an experience or a feeling at the altar more than he or she seeks the application of the Word of God on a daily basis, a real hindrance can occur.

It is important not to depend on the preacher at the altar or the feeling we get at the altar more than we depend on the Word of God. If we do, it could become a real obstacle to receiving true deliverance or healing from the Lord because God is a jealous God (see Exodus 20:5). He wants us to seek him more than an experience. When a saint comes to the altar over and over again for the same problems and still seems to be defeated, it could very well be that the individual is seeking an experience as opposed to seeking deliverance through faith and obedience to the Word of God. Consequently, ministers must teach individuals in their congregations to be careful not to make the experience or feeling at the altar into an idol. If ministers are not responsible in this area, they run the risk of producing lazy Christians who want a quick fix at the altar.

As previously pointed out, the Scripture proves that God still heals instantly through the laying on of hands. And I have also personally witnessed God bring great deliverance in a miraculous and instant fashion at the altar through the laying on of hands.

Again, the point to be made is that our dependence should be more so on the Lord and not on the vessel who performs the laying on of hands. Does this also imply that a minister should never lay hands on the same person more than once for the same problem? The purpose of this section entitled *Faith vs. Feeling* is not to develop a set of legalistic rules that prohibit a minister from laying hands on the same sick person more than once.

Mark 8:22-25, listed below, is an example of Jesus laying hands on the same blind man twice before the man received the full manifestation of his healing. Since we know that Jesus had a perfect anointing to heal the sick, we know that it was not a lack of faith on the part of Jesus that made it necessary for Jesus to lay hands twice. We can also safely conclude that Jesus knew that God the Father had honored the request to heal the man the first time. Jesus, our perfect example, apparently laid hands twice because the blind man in this example did not fully receive the miracle the first time the Lord laid hands. This example demonstrates that it is sometimes beneficial for a minister to go through a process of helping the sick to receive healing.

Mark 8:22-25 (NKJV)

And He came to Bethsaida; and they brought a blind man to Him, and begged Him to touch him. So He took the blind man by the hand and led him out of the town. And when He had spit on his eyes and put His hands on him, He asked him if he saw anything. And he looked up and said, "I see men like trees, walking." Then He put *His* hands again on his eyes again and made him look up. And he was restored and saw everyone clearly.

You might ask, "If I know Christ for myself, then why is it sometimes beneficial to have another believer lay hands on me for deliverance or healing?" The simple answer is that the New Testament gives us many examples of individuals getting healed after Paul, Peter, and other disciples laid hands on them. Mark 16:17-18 also says, "And these signs shall follow them that believe…they shall lay hands on the sick, and they shall recover." 1 Corinthians 12:9 mentions that the Lord gives "the gifts of healing" to some.

The Bible reminds us that there are times when a child of God can be so beat down by sickness and sin that it is necessary to have another person pray in order to restore spiritual and physical strength. James 5:14-16 is a specific Scripture that reminds us that God uses some of his servants to help others receive physical healing as well as deliverance over sin.

James 5:14-16

Is any sick among you? let him call for the elders of the church; and let them pray over him, anointing him with oil in the name of the Lord: And the prayer of faith *shall save the sick*, and the Lord *shall raise him up*; and if he have committed sins, they shall be *forgiven* him. *Confess your faults one to another, and pray one for another, that ye may be healed.* The effectual fervent prayer of a righteous man availeth much.

Oral Roberts wife Evelyn used to say, "Get under the spout where the glory comes out." In other words, you can sometimes receive your miracle through the hands of another person who is anointed by God.

But we also need to be reminded that Bosworth taught many individuals how to get healed without having hands laid on them. In fact, as we grow in faith, we can become less dependent on others, and more dependent on going to God directly for the healing that we need. Even if elders lay hands on us to impart healing, we still must hold on to God's healing promises for ourselves, or we can lose the blessing we received. There are also times when we must learn to go directly to God for our healing due to the fact that we will not have access to another anointed believer or elder.

Consequently, it is important to catch a balance. We should not grow so dependent on having hands laid on us to the point that we can never go to God for ourselves. On the other hand, we should not hesitate to allow another believer to lay hands on us for healing if the Lord leads us that way. It does not matter if you are 110 years old and have been following Christ for 100 years and have had hands laid on you 1,000 times for 900 different reasons. If God directs you to go to the altar to get hands laid on you again, do it. Never diminish or devalue the power of the ministry gifts that can come through the hands of another. But never forget that there are times when the Lord might choose not to deliver you through the hands of another. The Lord might simply want to deliver you directly through your own faith in Him so that you can avoid worshipping the gift more than the Giver.

Darlene Zschech, internationally acclaimed worship leader and writer of one of the world's most celebrated worship songs, "Shout To The Lord," points out that even in our worship services we must be careful not to worship the worship experience, not to worship the gift more than the Giver. Rather than trying to get everything we need in a feeling or experience, we must realize that everything we need is in the Word of God. If we simply trust in the good feelings we get in a worship or healing service, we will go home with no root in the Word and lose the victory because the feelings will go away.

If an individual puts more trust in the preacher's ability to lay hands on him than he puts in the Lord himself, it can sometimes create a roadblock that can prevent the person from being healed. The Lord may also deal with the preacher if his ministry influences people to grow too dependent upon experiences and feelings rather than the Word of God. I highly recommend the reading of *The Believer's Authority* by Kenneth Hagin as a book that will teach you to live in victory by walking in the authority of the Word of God as opposed to trusting in experiences or feelings.

In summary, the good feelings we can sometimes get from worshipping God or being prayed for at the altar can be wonderful and scriptural. But we must always seek to keep our feelings in proper perspective so that we do not lean too much on what we see or feel. **"For we walk by faith, not by sight" (2 Corinthians 5:7).**

As pointed out in a previous section, F. F. Bosworth taught that instead of just asking a minister to pray for us when we are in need of healing, it is more important for us to seek to be taught God's Word so that we can properly cooperate with God for our recovery.

Pastor Dutch Sheets, author of *Authority in Prayer: Praying in Power and Purpose*, testifies that several years ago he had warts all over his hands. In spite of the fact that he had everybody pray for him, he could not get his healing. He met with people who had the gift of healing and he was anointed with oil by elders, but he still couldn't get his breakthrough. Although there was nothing wrong with having others pray for him, he felt that the Lord was not manifesting the healing because God was calling him to a higher place. In essence, the Lord was saying, "Because I am a good Father, I'm not going to heal you through anybody else's prayers at this point in your spiritual journey because I expect more from you. I'm going to manifest your healing when you take the Word that I taught you and speak it over your life." Dutch took healing Scriptures and spoke them over his hands every day and within thirty days the warts were gone and his hands had brand new skin!

A DEMONSTRATION OF GOD'S POWER

The following Scriptures remind us that divine healings and other miracles are signs that separate Christianity from false religions:

Acts 4:29-30
And now, Lord, behold their threatenings: and grant unto thy servants, that with all boldness they may speak thy word, By stretching forth thine hand to heal; and that signs and wonders may be done by the name of thy holy child Jesus.

Acts 5:12
And by the hands of the apostles were many signs and wonders wrought among the people; (and they were all with one accord in Solomon's porch.

Acts 6:8
And Stephen, full of faith and power, did great wonders and miracles among the people.

PRAYING FOR UNBELIEVERS

Should I lay hands and pray for sick people who don't profess to believe in Christ or divine healing?

Modern day street preacher Todd White, a former drug addict and atheist who has been gifted by God with a special anointing for words of knowledge and healing, is a good example of the miracles that can take place when Christians are bold enough to pray for those who do not profess to believe in the healing power of God. He is known for his boldness in stepping out by faith to allow the power of God to touch strangers in places like Walmart.

According to CBN.com, "It is common for Todd to see dozens of people healed while he goes about his everyday life."

"This is every day for me," Todd said. "When I go to restaurants or if I go to the mall, or anywhere for that matter, Jesus paid a price for all. So all are in and all are a target for the love of God."

Although we realize that Jesus at times could not perform miracles because of unbelieving people (see Mark 6:5-6), there were times when the Lord set individuals free who were not in the place to believe for themselves. Obviously Lazarus could not have faith to be raised from the dead because he was already dead for three days when Jesus commanded him to come out of the grave! It was the Lord's faith alone that raised him from the dead. In Acts 14:9, a man who was crippled from birth jumped up and walked at Paul's command because Paul perceived "that he had faith to be healed." This lets us know that it is good to be led by the Spirit in terms of who we should pray for. There are times that people can get healed based primarily on our faith or their own faith, while at other times the Scriptures show us that people cannot receive miracles due to their own doubt or unbelief, in spite of the fact that someone with great faith is available to pray for them.

Although the Scripture clearly teaches that doubt can be a hindrance to receiving a miracle from God, Todd White emphasizes the point that we should not focus on an individual's lack of faith when we are praying for their healing. He points out that *these signs shall follow those who believe, not those being prayed for*. And Todd often prays for non-Christians who do not understand divine healing, because he believes his faith can trump their unbelief.

A good example of Todd's ability to reach individuals from all backgrounds was demonstrated when Todd prayed for a man on the street who was a bartender. The young man had been shot in his right eye with a pellet gun and was about 50 percent blind in that eye. The man's vision was miraculously restored after Todd finished praying for him on the street and the entire event was filmed and televised on *The 700 Club*. This is how the incident unfolded: Todd laid hands on the young man's right eye and also asked the man's friend who was with him to lay his hand on the eye and repeat the prayer as well. Below is a partial transcript of the conversation, starting off with Todd's prayer as he laid his hand on the man's right eye.

Todd: "Jesus we thank you for a brand new eye. Eye we command you see right now…100 percent…Eye open…in Jesus name.

"Open your eye," he asks the young man after a few moments of silence

Man on the Street: "Significantly better…It really is."

Todd: "It's gonna be 100 percent. Lets pray again."

Man on the Street: "It is?"

Todd: "Yeah Dude? Are you kiddin' me. This is Jesus. He's like…amazing…Let's pray again. Lord thank you in Jesus name. We've had 50 percent…We're at 80 percent…and we're thanking you for a finished job…eye open…in Jesus name."

Todd: "Open it," he asks the young man again.

Man on the Street: "Much better. It really is."

Todd: "What's up dude? What are you seeing?"

Man on the Street: "I'm seeing almost full vision right now."

Todd: "Right on dude. So it's not completely full yet?"

Man on the Street: "No, not yet."

Todd: "Come on man, one more time…All right let's do this again. In Jesus name…eye we command you…open…right now…full vision."

"Open it up," he asks the young man again after a few moments of silence.

Man on the Street: "You kidding me. You kidding me right now," the man says in total awe as his very own vision has been restored on the spot!

Todd: "No dude. It's your eye, what do you see? It's 100 percent."

Man on the Street: "It really is."

Todd: "I guarantee that it is."

Man on the Street: "Wow."

Todd: "So check this out…you got shot in the eye…how long ago?"

Man on the Street: "2004."

Todd: "2004 with what?"

Man on the Street: "A pellet gun."

Todd: "A pellet gun in your eye…and you've had 50 percent vision and it's a hundred percent right now."

Man on the Street: "It really is."

Todd: "What do you think of that?"

Man on the Street: "I think it's unbelievable."

Todd: "That's amazing…Jesus so loves you. You're amazing."

Man on the Street: "He does. I know he does."

Todd: "100 percent."

Man on the Street: "100 percent…I'm amazed. I really am…I can't believe that."

Todd: "It's your eye you gotta believe it. You're seeing out of it," he says with joyful laughter.

Note that it took three times for Todd to pray for the young man before he got full restoration of his vision. Todd says that some people have been incorrectly taught to only pray for something once, but we should persistently speak to the mountain until it moves.

In the beginning of his ministry, Todd started out day after day praying for the sick with no results—hundreds of people over three and a half months. Now he is surprised if he prays and the sick person doesn't get healed. Admitting that he still doesn't see everybody he prays for healed, Todd believes that more Christians ought to be willing to risk stepping out to pray for the sick with more boldness, even if the results aren't always manifested right away.

Todd's home base is in Abbottstown, Pennsylvania, where he is a ministry leader and teacher. Todd has not only been blessed to travel domestically seeing miracles, but on a pilgrimage to Jerusalem, he saw over 150 Muslims and Jews healed by the power of God through the name of Jesus Christ on the streets.

RECEIVING SPIRITUAL HEALING FROM THE SINS OF THE PAST

The Bible teaches in James chapter 5 that we can sometimes receive spiritual and physical healing by confessing our faults to one another. In other words, in some cases it is important for us to first deal with our sins before we attempt to receive physical healing.

I have also discovered that people can even be oppressed with certain physical ailments or sinful addictions due to generational issues. If you are a born again believer, however, generational sins or sicknesses have no right to oppress you. You can decree something like: "I appropriate the cross of Christ and the blood of Jesus between me and any generational issues. I decree that generational sins or sicknesses have no right to oppress me or my family because I have been washed in the blood of the Lamb and with His stripes I am already healed."

The Bible also reminds us that Christians who commit certain types of immoral acts open up the door to spiritual or physical oppression. In the verses below, the Apostle Paul was addressing the issue of immorality in the church and explaining how ungodly, sexual soul ties are formed when sexual sins are committed:

1 Corinthians 6:15-20 NKJV
Do you not know that your bodies are members of Christ? Shall I then take the members of Christ and make *them* members of a harlot? Certainly not! Or do you not know that he who is joined to a harlot is one body *with her?* For *"the two,"* He says, *"shall become one flesh."* But he who is joined to the Lord is one spirit *with Him.* Flee sexual immorality. Every sin that a man does is outside the body, but he who commits sexual immorality sins against his own body. Or do you not know that your body is the temple of the Holy Spirit *who is* in you, whom you have from God, and

you are not your own? For you were bought at a price; therefore glorify God in your body and in your spirit, which are God's.

If you are a Christian who has slipped back into a pattern of sin, Scriptures like the ones above help you to gain an understanding of the need to break the consequences of ungodly soul ties (sexual or nonsexual). You can do this by specifically confessing and renouncing your sins. If things like anger and lust ran through your family tree and happen to be your weaknesses as well, you might need to sever these ungodly ties. I encourage you to say a prayer similar to the one below:

> Father God, in the name of Jesus, I confess and repent of the sin of an ungodly soul tie(s) with (name a specific person or persons). I also forgive myself for practicing these sins and I forgive (name a specific person or persons) as well. I ask you to break the ungodly soul tie(s) with (name a specific person or persons) and I ask you to bring full restoration to my soul where I have been broken and damaged by sin. Lord, I ask you to replace good things that have been stolen from me as a result of my sins and ungodly soul ties, and I also ask you to remove anything harmful that has been added to me. And I thank you for the grace, strength, and wisdom that will keep me from formulating ungodly soul ties in the future. In the name of Jesus. Amen

I encourage you to sincerely pray the above prayers if lust or some other sin has been defeating you over and over again. These prayers can help you to receive the full deliverance or spiritual healing that you need.

It is important to remember that we were healed from "sin sickness" by the same means that we were healed physically. **"But he was wounded for our transgressions, he was bruised for our iniquities: the chastisement of our peace was upon him; and with his stripes we are healed"** (Isaiah 53:5). Consequently, it is important to accept the healing that the Lord already paid the price for on the cross. And one way we accept the healing is by making sure that our words are in line with the Word of God. This means we can say, "Thank you Lord that I am free" (after repenting) or "Thank you Lord that I am healed" even before the manifestation of the deliverance fully takes place.

If you think about it, a lot of our defeats in life come from wrong thinking and lack of discipline due to wrong habits. The Bible says, "For as he thinketh in his heart, so is he" (Proverbs 23:7). It also tells us that we must discipline the body and "bring it into subjection" (1 Corinthians 9:27). If we can change our negative thinking to positive thinking while we replace our bad habits with good habits, we can gain the victory.

HEALING AND THE AGING PROCESS

Is it every Christian's privilege to have his eyes preserved so that he never needs to wear glasses?"

Since I have not yet come across any research in which Bosworth addressed this issue, I will refer to the writings of one of Bosworth's contemporaries, Smith Wigglesworth, to answer this question. Smith Wigglesworth (1859-1947) was one of several British evangelists who made tours of the United States in the 1920s and 1930s. A plumber by trade in England, by the 1920s he had become a prominent healing revivalist. "When in America," recalled Pentecostal editor Stanley Frodsham, "he filled the biggest halls, ministered to record crowds, prayed for thousands of people." Thousands came to Christian faith in his meetings and thousands were healed of serious illnesses and diseases as supernatural signs followed his ministry. About 20 people were reportedly raised from the dead after he prayed for them.

Wigglesworth died in 1947, but he left behind some powerful writings that have served as a guide for the next generation of revivalists. In the book entitled *Smith Wigglesworth on Healing* (Published by Whitaker House, New Kensington, PA), Wigglesworth answered the question, *Is it every Christian's privilege to have his eyes preserved so that he never needs to wear glasses?*

> *"The aging process affects every person...I see that many are here today with gray hair and white hair; this shows that the natural man decays, and you cannot do what you like with it...However, although the natural man has had a change, I believe and affirm that the supernatural power can be so ministered to us that even our eyesight can be preserved right through...*
>
> *"I have been preaching faith to my people for thirty years. When my daughter came back from Africa and saw her mother and me with glasses, she was amazed. When our people saw*

us put glasses on the first time, they were very troubled. They were no more troubled than we were. But I found it was far better to be honest with the people and acknowledge my condition than get a Bible with large print and deceive the people and say that my eyesight was all right. I like to be honest.

"My eyesight gave way at about age fifty-three, and somehow God is doing something. I am now sixty-eight, and I do not need a stronger prescription than I needed then, and I am satisfied that God is restoring me...My eyes will be restored, but until then, I will not deceive anybody. I will wear glasses until I can see perfectly...

"Often I pray for a person's eyesight, and as soon as he is prayed for, he believes, and God stimulates his faith, but his eyesight is about the same. 'What should I do?' he asks. 'Should I go without any glasses?'

"'Can you see perfectly?' I ask. 'Do you need any help?'

"'Yes. If I were to go without my glasses, I would stumble.'

"'Put your glasses on,' I say, 'for when your faith is perfected, you will no longer need your glasses. When God perfects your faith, your glasses will drop off. But as long as you need them, use them.'

"You can take that for what you like, but I believe in common sense."

I am in full agreement with Smith Wigglesworth about this issue of common sense because I have personally done some unwise things in the name of faith—things that lacked common sense.

What Smith Wigglesworth reminds us of here is that developing our faith to a higher level is a process. We should not be so quick to condemn others or to condemn ourselves just because we do not become giants of faith overnight. Just like we engage in battle we must engage the Word. This is what Cheryl, Nasir and the Ooman family did in the testimonies we shared in the beginning of this book. They did not accept their circumstances, but they consistently spoke the Word over their situation until they saw manifested results.

I fully agree with a statement I once heard from a preacher. The preacher said that if you wear glasses and you want to believe God to improve your vision so that you will not need glasses anymore, it is better to keep wearing your glasses while you are trusting God for better vision. Rather than be presumptuous and stop wearing your glasses before your vision improves, the preacher explained that it is better to continue believing until one day you notice that you no longer need your glasses. Then you can stop wearing them.

Another thing to consider about the issue of glasses is that having less than perfect vision is not a life-threatening situation. And having a pair of glasses or contact lenses is a remedy that corrects vision. Consequently, it is common for even people of faith to take the easier way out and rely on the glasses or contact lenses rather than put forth the effort of engaging God's Word. This obviously is not as good as having perfect vision without the aid of glasses or contact lenses, but it is certainly a good solution for better vision.

On the other hand, man's extremity is God's opportunity. In an emergency situation when an optometrist or doctor can do nothing for us is when we are more likely to engage in spiritual warfare for a supernatural healing. Obviously, the more serious or life-threatening a situation is, the more we need to engage the Word. If a person is diagnosed with cancer, for example, and only given six months to live, it is much more important for that individual to engage in spiritual battle by speaking, reading, hearing and acting upon the Word. Sometimes we can engage a little bit when we should be engaging a lot. If you have a headache, you might only have to engage a little bit. If you wear glasses but would like your vision improved to the point that you no longer need glasses, and you fail to engage the way you need to, it will not cost you your life. You simply will have to continue wearing glasses. But with a life-threatening disease like cancer, you would engage a lot. You must stay engaged until the answer comes.

I once heard a testimony about a minister who was diagnosed with a life-threatening form of cancer. The minister was so serious about getting victory over the cancer through his faith in God that he pulled out all stops in order to engage in battle. Not only did he constantly read, speak, listen to, and apply Scriptures specifically related to healing, but he even went as far as canceling some of his speaking engagements so that he could fast and pray and focus more on winning his personal battle over cancer. As a result of his relentless attitude of faith and perseverance, the minister was completely healed of the cancer!

In addition to understanding the need to engage in battle in order to overcome sickness and disease, the Scriptures remind us that God's children can also live in divine health on a continual basis:

Psalm 105:37
He brought them forth also with silver and gold: and there was not one feeble person among their tribes.

Also, the life of Moses reminds us that in spite of the fact that there is an aging process, it is still possible to defy the odds and maintain great health or excellent vision even in old age:

Deuteronomy 34:7 NKJV
Moses was one hundred and twenty years old when he died. His eyes were not dim nor his natural vigor diminished.

ARE YOU EXERCISING FAITH OR ARE YOU BEING FOOLISH?

On his "Ever Increasing Faith" television program, pastor and teacher Frederick K. C. Price taught a very prolific and practical message titled *Faith, Foolishness, and Presumption*. In this classic message from many years ago—which is still available through the ministry website—Dr. Price proclaimed that faith is acting on the Word of God and that you must be a doer of the Word. On the other hand, he explained that some Christians do foolish or presumptuous things while attempting to exercise faith. Dr. Price defined foolishness as deficiency in understanding, exhibiting folly, without judgment or discretion, silly, unwise, witless, or irrational. Presumption, he explained, means to take for granted, to suppose, or to assume a thing is true without any evidence.

Dr. Price further explained that some Christians think that having things like medical insurance or taking medication is a sign that a person is not operating in faith, but things like medical insurance or medication are irrelevant and immaterial unless you put your faith in these things. In other words, to have or not to have insurance doesn't mean you do or don't have faith, and we should not try to put people in bondage by telling them that they do not have faith if they have medical insurance, take medication, etc.

If I seek medical help or take medicine or wear glasses, does that mean that I am not operating in faith? Not necessarily so, says Dr. Price, explaining that some people have misconceptions and feel that if you have faith you can't take medicine, or you should get rid of your glasses if you are believing God to restore your vision. The Bible does not imply anywhere that taking medicine is in contradiction to divine healing, says Dr. Price. The purpose of medicine is to get you better, so in some cases taking medicine can be in line with the Word of God concerning improving your health.

In addition to the things Dr. Price mentioned concerning medicine, I would also like to remind believers that it is not foolish to decide not to take medication in certain instances—as long as you are not operating in the type of presumption or foolishness described by Dr. Price. In other words, if a doctor is giving a person the option of having an operation or taking medication that could do much more harm than good because of certain side effects, then it is understandable why a believer in a situation like this would decide to trust in God and forfeit the medical treatment. As Dr. Price warned in his message, however, individuals must be careful not to deny themselves or others of medical treatment when it could lead to an unnecessary fatality.

If, on the other hand, you have avoided presumption and foolishness and have also excelled in your faith and lifestyle choices to the point where you constantly walk in divine health and healing without the need for any type of medication, this is indeed a commendable accomplishment. The key is to avoid the type of extreme foolishness and presumption that leads to the type of unnecessary suffering that does not glorify the Lord.

Dr. Price told a story about a tragic case of presumption where a diabetic child died because his presumptuous parents refused to let him continue taking his insulin. God was not glorified through this tragic experience caused by presumptuous parents who believed they were operating in faith. Taking insulin, Dr. Price explained, does not necessarily mean you do not have faith. It simply might mean that you are utilizing medical help to work in concert with the Word of God to improve your health until your healing is manifested to the point where you no longer need the insulin. It is the same as wearing glasses until your healing is manifested to the point where you no longer need the glasses.

According to Dr. Price, there are miracle healings (sometimes instant) and there are faith healings (typically a process) in which a person receives healing by exercising faith or standing on the Word of God. It might take time for the healing to manifest, but the seed of faith must be watered with your verbal confession of faith in spite of any symptoms to the contrary. In the meantime, you might still need the glasses or the insulin because the healing has not fully manifested.

In many cases, it is sensible to wear the glasses or take the insulin if you need it until you receive the manifestation of the healing. Faith is the evidence, not the fact that you don't wear glasses or don't take insulin. Dr. Price says every time you put those glasses on in the morning or take that insulin, you can say "Praise God, I believe I am healed" and still not be inconsistent regarding your faith.

Another true story Dr. Price told was about two men with diabetes—a young man and an elderly man—who had both heard some teaching about divine healing. The young man declared that he would trust God or die, so he threw his insulin away, went into insulin shock and died! The older man grasped the understanding and would take his insulin while saying "Father, I believe that I am healed." One day while driving, the older gentleman had a car accident and went to the doctor to get examined. His doctor informed him that he was not seriously injured regarding the accident, but the examination also revealed that he no longer had diabetes and did not need to take the insulin anymore! The presumptuous young man died prematurely because he assumed he had to stop taking medication in order to prove he had faith. The older man experienced divine healing because he kept believing and speaking the Word of faith while he was taking his medication.

The final true story Dr. Price told was in reference to a woman with very bad vision who had stopped wearing her glasses after she heard a message about faith and divine healing. This well-meaning woman with extremely poor eyesight wrongly assumed that she had to risk her life driving without her glasses in order to prove she was operating in faith. Her presumption and foolishness could have caused her to kill herself or someone else, but fortunately a sensible minister advised her to wear her glasses daily while she simply confessed, "I believe that I'm healed." For six long months the woman did this, until one day she put her glasses on and discovered that her vision was extremely blurred with the glasses, but had been totally restored without the glasses. She was healed!

SIX TYPES OF PRAYER

Gaining an understanding of the six different types of prayer listed below will help you to better understand how to pray appropriately for healing as opposed to praying for guidance or something else.

1) The Prayer of Agreement

Matthew 18:19
Again I say unto you, That if two of you shall agree on earth as touching any thing that they shall ask, it shall be done for them of my Father which is in heaven.

You must first make sure that you are on the same page (in full agreement) with the other individual you are praying with in order to get the full benefits of this type of prayer. For example, if you are praying for God to supernaturally heal someone of sickness, you do not need to be praying with a person who is not fully convinced that it is God's will (according to His Word) to heal. When two or more people pray together in total agreement, there is more power and authority added to the prayer. Agreement is also important because God will not violate the will of an unbelieving person. Also, according to John 16:23-24, we should ask the Father in the name of the Son when we pray.

2) The Prayer of Faith or Prayer of Petition

Mark 11:24
Therefore I say unto you, What things soever ye desire, when ye pray, believe that ye receive them, and ye shall have them.

When you pray the prayer of faith, you must know God's will in the matter (according to His Word) and you must believe God has answered your prayer before the answer is fully manifested. This means that after you pray the prayer of faith, you don't have to keep asking God for the same thing over and over again. But you can continually thank Him for answering your prayer even before the answer is fully manifested in the natural. Also, when you pray this type of prayer, you never say, "If it be your will, Lord."

3) The Prayer of Consecration and Dedication

Luke 22:41-42
And he was withdrawn from them about a stone's cast, and kneeled down, and prayed, Saying, Father, if thou be willing, remove this cup from me: nevertheless not my will, but thine, be done.

When you pray this type of prayer, it is appropriate to say, "If it be your will, Lord" because you might need God to show you what city to move to, what church to join, or what job to take. Like Jesus in Luke 22, you might be exploring different options to solve the problem, but ultimately you will pray, "Nevertheless not my will, but your will be done."

4) The Prayer of Praise and Worship

John 11:41
Then they took away the stone from the place where the dead was laid. And Jesus lifted up his eyes, and said, Father, I thank thee that thou hast heard me.

With this type of prayer, you don't ask the Lord for anything, but you simply thank Him in the name of Jesus, or you thank Him in faith knowing that the answer to a previous prayer you prayed is on the way.

5) The Prayer of Intercession

Philippians 1:3-4
I thank my God upon every remembrance of you, Always in every prayer of mine for you all making request with joy...

Intercession is praying on behalf of someone else or "standing in the gap," so to speak, for individuals who might not be able to pray for themselves. You might intercede for the troops, for example, or you might intercede for a specific person who is sick, who needs a job, or is bound by drugs. It is best to pray right away when you feel the need to intercede for someone. In 1 Corinthians 14:13-15, Paul mentions prayer that involves praying with the spirit (in other tongues) and praying with understanding. In Romans 8:26-27, Paul also mentions a type of intercessory prayer that involves praying with the Spirit. This is a means of praying a perfect prayer even though you don't know specifically what you should pray for.

6) The Prayer of Binding and Loosing

Matthew 18:18-19
Verily I say unto you, Whatsoever ye shall bind on earth shall be bound in heaven: and whatsoever ye shall loose on earth shall be loosed in heaven.

According to God's laws or promises, you can bind evil, demonic forces or loose angelic spirits. In essence, when we take action on earth through prayer, heaven follows suit and "backs us up." You can pray something like, "Satan, I bind you in the name of Jesus from tormenting this person and I loose them from this oppression in the name of Jesus."

POINTS TO PONDER

- Because "faith cometh by hearing" (Romans 10:17), read the healing Scriptures in the Bible, read this book over and over, and listen to healing Scriptures and healing messages in audio format over and over in order to build stronger faith for healing. This practice can be extremely beneficial for those who are sick and also for those who are not sick who simply want to be knowledgeable enough to help others or to be prepared for any future needs.

- As far as I can tell according to my research, Bosworth was a very balanced theologian who also understood that God sometimes used doctors as a part of our healing process. Balance is the key. It does not necessarily mean that a Christian does not have faith because he or she follows the advice of a sensible doctor or takes medication while believing God for the full manifestation of the healing. The key is not to trust in the earthly physician more than we trust in Christ; it is understanding that Jesus is the Great Physician who can help us when the doctor can do no more. It is also important for the individual to be very prayerful and conscious of avoiding presumption regarding whether or not to take certain types of medications or how long to take them. I know of cases in which Christians have gotten totally healed of certain conditions after deciding not to use medical assistance. This is fine as long as the person has the faith to believe and is also led of the Lord. I also know of a tragic situation in which a man refused to take his baby to a doctor because he felt that God was going to heal the baby without any medical assistance. Unfortunately, the baby died. This was a real tragedy because God could have blessed that family by using a doctor to save the life of the baby. **In Psalm 19:13, David prayed, "Keep back thy servant also from presumptuous sins; let them not have dominion over me."** The healing process can be assisted by natural means through a doctor or with medication, but always remember that ultimately God is Jehovah-Rapha—"I am the Lord that healeth thee" or "I am the Lord thy Physician."

- As much as possible, protect the sick person from the person or minister who speaks or prays faith-destroying words. David Yonggi Cho, pastor of the largest church in the world in Seoul, Korea, points out that it is extremely important that in group prayer we block all unbelief from being manifested. In his church, he first builds faith through Bible study and teaching before joining together in group prayer. In his book entitled *Prayer That Brings Revival*, Cho says, "Just as faith builds power in prayer, unbelief destroys that power. It is like a cancer that must be cut out completely!" Referring to the passage where Jesus put the doubters out (see Mark 5:37-40), Cho also points out that if Jesus was careful about whom he allowed to pray with Him, we should also be careful.

- Admonish the sick person to make sure that he is right with God (saved and forgiven by the grace of God).

- Just as a person preaching salvation is not pressured if a hearer of the Word goes through the motions of repentance and baptism but does not genuinely become born again, a person praying for the sick should not be pressured about what critics might say if the person who is sick isn't healed. Sometimes people can fail to receive healing, but this does not mean that God is not willing to heal. In the same manner, God is not willing that any should perish concerning eternal salvation, but unfortunately there are many who will perish due to their unbelief. One should not claim that it is God's fault or responsibility if individuals are not saved or healed.

- Bosworth recommended that as our first prayer every day we ask the Lord to quicken us (give us more life) according to his Word (see Psalm119:25).

- Make sure that the person who is sick understands that at Calvary disease and sin were cancelled (see 1 Peter 2:24).

- Get filled with the Spirit to further stimulate faith.

- Be aware that we can lose the blessing of the healing that God gave to us if we fail to continuously walk in his principles.

- Could disobedience in financial giving according to God's Word be a hindrance to a person's faith in reference to receiving God's healing power? Malachi 3:8-12 indicates that even our obedience in financial giving will cause the Lord to "rebuke the devourer" and open the "windows of heaven." This is certainly not to imply that we should try to pay for a miracle. But disobedience in the area of finances could be an indication that a person has not fully surrendered everything to the Lord. "For where your treasure is, there will your heart be also" (Matthew 6:21). I must emphasize, however, that the focus should not be about your works. Regardless of what you have or have not done in the past, simply ask God to forgive you and to show you mercy, then believe the Lord for your deliverance.

Malachi 3:8-12

Will a man rob God? Yet ye have robbed me. But ye say, Wherein have we robbed thee? In tithes and offerings. Ye _are_ cursed with a curse: for ye have robbed me, _even_ this whole nation. Bring ye all the tithes into the storehouse, that there may be meat in mine house, and prove me now herewith, saith the LORD of hosts, if I will not open you the windows of heaven, and pour you out a blessing, that _there shall_ not _be room_ enough _to receive it._ And I will rebuke the devourer for your sakes, and he shall not destroy the fruits of your ground; neither shall your vine cast her fruit before the time in the field, saith the LORD of hosts. And all nations shall call you blessed: for ye shall be a delightsome land, saith the LORD of hosts.

- **What about Christians who are struggling with smoking or other habits that could lead to cancer or other illnesses?** It is important that we encourage and teach these individuals to apply the Word of faith in order to overcome such bad habits before they lead to illness. If a Christian learns to kick a habit such as smoking, it will be easier for the same individual to overcome greater trials in the future if his body is attacked with sickness or disease.

- Some children are angry or confused about God or embittered against God because people have told them things like, "God took your mommy away. She died of cancer because it was the Lord's will to take her home." This might sound good and spiritual to some, but Jesus never denied anyone of his healing, and neither did he ever imply that it was the will of the Father to "take someone home" with sickness or disease. I will point out, however, that God can allow sickness to take a person to heaven now in order to save them from hell later. As Pastor Dutch Sheets once pointed out, God knows that if some people get healed, their seeds of rebellion will cause them to backslide and wind up in hell. Consequently, Pastor Sheets points out that one of the keys to successful prayer is learning to listen to the Holy Spirit. He recalls an experience in which the Lord spoke to him and let him know that one man he was praying for would make it while another would not make it. If a Christian dies from sickness, it is not wrong to say that he or she died and went home to be with the Lord, but we should be very careful to avoid giving our children explanations about sickness and death that could cause them to wrongly blame God. The Word of God makes it clear that the devil is the devourer and Christ is the one who heals those who are oppressed by the devil:

1 Peter 5:8
Be sober, be vigilant; because your adversary the devil, as a roaring lion, walketh about, seeking whom he may devour.

John 10:10
The thief cometh not, but for to steal, and to kill, and to destroy; I am come that they might have life, and that they might have it more abundantly.

Acts 10:38
How God anointed Jesus of Nazareth with the Holy Ghost and with power: who went about doing good, and healing all that were oppressed of the devil; for God was with him.

1 John 3:8
For this purpose the Son of God was manifested, that he might destroy the works of the devil.

- Consider the importance of persistent faith as demonstrated by the Canaanite woman in Matthew 15:22-28. This is one of Jesus' few known dealings with a Gentile. The woman, who pleaded with the Lord to have mercy for the sake of her demon-possessed daughter, was told by the Lord that it was not good "to take the children's bread, and to cast it to dogs" (v. 26). Perhaps the Lord's intention was to make the unregenerated woman aware of her state of being to get her in position to receive. Jesus' reply was not a cold-hearted rejection but a test of the woman's humility and faith. The Lord is referring to Jews when he says "children," and he is referring to heathens or individuals not grafted into the covenant when he mentions dogs. Dogs (in Greek, *kuhariois*) in this context also means "little dogs," household pets as opposed to wild beasts. The Canaanite woman somehow knew that by faith she could receive miraculous help from the Lord, and she became a testimony to people of all races, colors, and creeds concerning the Lord's willingness to deliver all who come with humility and persistent faith. Although Jesus explained to the woman that his primary purpose at the time was to "the lost sheep of the house of Israel," the Jews (v. 24), the Gentile woman caught the Lord's attention because of her great faith and persistence.

Matthew 15:22-28 (NKJV)
And behold, a woman of Canaan came from that region and cried out to Him, saying, "Have mercy on me, O Lord, Son of David! My daughter is severely demon-possessed." But He answered her not a word. And His disciples came and urged Him, saying, "Send her away, for she cries out after us." But He answered and said, I was not sent except to the lost sheep of the house of Israel. Then she came and worshiped Him, saying, "Lord, help me!" But He answered and said, "It is not good to take the children's bread and throw *it* to the little dogs." And she said, "Yes, Lord, yet even the

little dogs eat the crumbs which fall from the masters' table." Then Jesus answered and said to her, O woman, great is your faith! Let it be to you as you desire. And her daughter was healed from that very hour.

- When praying for others, consider the importance of being led by the spirit to especially recognize those who have faith to be healed. When your faith connects with the faith of another, it creates a greater opportunity for God to work a miracle. In Matthew 9:27-30, the two blind men asked Jesus to have mercy on them because they wanted to receive their sight. Jesus asked them, "Do you believe that I am able to do this?" They said to him, "Yes, Lord." Then Jesus touched their eyes, saying, "According to your faith let it be to you." And their eyes were opened. This scriptural example demonstrates that even Jesus, the perfect Son of God, often connected his faith with the faith of others in order to manifest miracles. The following Scripture from the book of Acts shows another illustration of faith connecting with faith, using the Apostle Paul and a crippled man as an example.

Acts 14:8-10 (NKJV)
And in Lystra a certain man without strength in his feet was sitting, a cripple from his mother's womb, who had never walked. This man heard Paul speaking. Paul, observing him intently and seeing that he had faith to be healed, said with a loud voice, "Stand up straight on your feet!" And he leaped and walked.

A SAMPLE PRAYER FOR THE SICK THAT YOU CAN USE

I do not profess to be an expert on how to pray for sickness, but below is a basic prayer I came up with based on some of the principles in this book. I encourage you not to view this prayer as a strict formula, but to simply use it as a basic guideline. There are many great ministers who have dealt with the topic of how to pray for the sick in books or in live teaching sessions. I encourage you to do all you can to learn from other credible ministers whenever the Lord leads you to do so. But for now, here is a sample prayer I came up with that might be helpful to you:

Lord, I first ask You to forgive me of all my sins and transgressions right now and show me how to overcome any hindrance to receiving the manifestation of my healing.

In the midst of this sickness that has come against me, I ask You to have mercy on me and let Your healing virtue be fully manifested in me. And I thank You that Micah 7:18 lets me know that You delight in mercy, and I receive Your mercy right now.

I thank You that You were wounded for my transgressions and bruised for my iniquities and with Your stripes I am already healed (according to Isaiah 53:5), because You already paid the price and it is Your desire to heal me. So I fully receive the gift of healing You have provided for me through Your blood sacrifice.

Thank You, Lord, that I am healed and I receive Your healing virtue right now in spite of any symptoms of sickness I might see or feel. Thank You, Lord, in advance for the total manifestation of my healing, for I walk by faith and not by sight according to 2 Corinthians 5:7. I receive Your mercy and I command this sickness to leave my body and I command my body to be made well right now in the name of Jesus!

APPENDIX

While praying the above prayer, it might even be a good idea to touch the part of your body that needs healing with your own hand and mention that part of your body specifically. You can also modify the above prayer slightly and pray it for others or teach others to pray it themselves.

THIRTY-ONE QUESTIONS
By F. F. Bosworth

THIRTY-ONE QUESTIONS, propounded by evangelist F. F. Bosworth in the Alliance Tabernacle, Toronto, Canada, April 20, 1923, as a part of his sermon answering the question "Is there a gospel of healing?"

1. Since the seven compound names of Jehovah, one of which is Jehovah-Rapha (I am the Lord that healeth thee), reveal His redemptive relationship toward each person, do they not point to Calvary?

2. Since all the promises of God are yea and amen in Him, do not these seven names, including Jehovah-Rapha (the Lord our Healer), owe their existence and their power to the redeeming work of Christ on the cross?

3. Has not every believer the same redemptive right to call upon Christ as Jehovah-Rapha (the Healer of his body) as he has to call upon Him as Jehovah-Tsidkenu (the Healer of his soul)? Is not His name given for healing as long as it is for salvation?

4. If bodily healing is to be obtained independent of Calvary, as opposers teach, why was it that no blessing of the Year of Jubilee was to be announced by the sounding of the trumpet until the Day of Atonement?

5. If healing for the body was not a part of Christ's redeeming work, why were types of the Atonement given in connection with healing throughout the Old Testament?

6. If healing was not in the Atonement, why were the dying Israelites required to look at the type of the Atonement for bodily healing? If both forgiveness and healing came by a look at the type, why not from the antitype?

7. Since their curse was removed by the lifting up of the type of Christ, was not our curse a disease also removed by the lifting up of Christ Himself? (Galatians 3:13)

8. In the passage, "Surely He hath borne our sicknesses and carried our pains" (Isaiah 53:4), why are the same Hebrew verbs for "borne" and "carried" employed as are used in verses 11 and 12 for the substitutionary bearing of sin unless they have the same substitutionary and expiatory character?

9. If healing was not provided for all in redemption, how did the multitudes obtain from Christ what God did not provide?

10. If the body was not included in redemption, how can there be a resurrection or how can corruption put on incorruption or mortality put on immortality? Were not the physical as well as the spiritual earnests (foretastes) of our coming redemption enjoyed by God's people throughout history?

11. Why should not the second Adam take away all that the first Adam brought upon us?

12. Since the Church is the body of Christ, does God want the body of Christ sick? Is it not His will to heal any part of the body of Christ? If not, why does He command "any sick" in it to be anointed for healing?

13. Are human imperfections of any sort, be they physical or moral, God's will or are they man's mistakes?

14. Since "the body is for the Lord, a living sacrifice unto God" would He not rather have a well body than a wrecked one? If not, how can He make us "perfect in every good work to do His will" or have us "thoroughly furnished unto every good work?"

15. Since bodily healing in the New Testament was called a mercy and it was mercy and compassion that moved Jesus to heal all

who came to Him, is not the promise of God still true, "He is plenteous in Mercy unto all that call upon Him?"

16. Does not the glorious Gospel dispensation offer as much mercy and compassion to its sufferers as did the darker dispensations? If not, why would God withdraw this mercy and this Old Testament privilege from a better dispensation with its "better Covenant?"

17. If, as some teach, God has another method for our healing today, why would God adopt a less successful method for our better dispensation?

18. Since Christ came to do the Father's will, was not the universal healing of all the sick who came to Him a revelation of the will of God for our bodies?

19. Did not Jesus emphatically say that He would continue His same works in answer to our prayers while He is with the Father (John 14:12-13) and is not this promise alone a complete answer to all opposers?

20. Why would the Holy Spirit, who healed all the sick before His dispensation began, do less after He entered into office on the day of Pentecost? Or did the Miracle-Worker enter office to do away with miracles?

21. Is not the book of the Acts of the Holy Ghost a revelation of the way He wants to continue to act through the Church?

22. How can God justify us and at the same time require us to remain under the curse of the law which Jesus redeemed us from by bearing it for us on the cross? (Galatians 3:13)

23. Since "The Son of God was manifested that He might destroy the works of the devil," has He now relinquished this purpose which He retained even during the bloody sweat of Gethsemane and the tortures of Calvary? Or does He now want the works of the devil in our bodies to continue that He formerly wanted to destroy? Does God want a cancer,—"a plague," "a curse"—"the works of the devil" in the members of Christ? "Know ye not that your bodies are the members of Christ?" (I Corinthians 6:15)

24. Are the proofs of Divine Healing among the one hundred and eighty-four persons who testified in this Tabernacle the last two Friday nights, less bright and convincing than the proofs of Spiritual Redemption among professed Christians today? Are not these 184 who have been healed in better health physically than a like number of professed Christians are spiritually? Would not the physical health of these 184 compare favorably with the spiritual health of even the same number of ministers of our day?

25. Would not the argument commonly employed against Divine Healing, drawn from its failures, if employed against justification, regeneration and all the rest be simply overwhelming?

26. Does the fact that Christ could do no miracle at Nazareth prove anything except the unbelief of the people, or would it be right to conclude, because of the failure of Christ's disciples to cast out the epileptic spirit from the boy, that it was not God's will to deliver him? Christ proved by healing him that it is God's will to heal even those who fail to receive it.

27. Is not God as willing to show the mercy of healing to His worshipers as He is to show the mercy of forgiveness to His enemies? (Romans 8:32)

28. If Paul (as a New York minister says) "was the sickest of men suffering from ophthalmia of the eyes," or if, as others teach, his "thorn in the flesh" was physical weakness instead of what Paul himself says it was, "Satan's angel" inflicting the many buffetings which Paul enumerates, how could he labor more abundantly than all the other apostles? Or since he had strength to do more work than all the others, how could his "weaknesses" be physical? Since Paul's "thorn" did not hinder His faith for the universal healing of "all the rest of the sick folk on the Island" of Melita, (Moffatt's trans.), why should it hinder ours? Would not Paul's failure to be healed, if he was sick, hinder the universal faith of these heathen for their healing? Why do traditional teachers substitute "ophthalmia of the eyes" or sickness (neither of which Paul mentions) for the "reproaches," "necessities," "persecutions," "distresses" and all the other buffetings at the

hands of "Satan's angels" which he does mention. If the former constitute his "thorn," why does he not say he takes pleasure in the former instead of the latter? How could Paul, sick in body, or with the unsightly disease of "ophthalmia of the eyes," and unable to be healed, "make the Gentiles obedient by word and deed through mighty signs and wonders?" (Romans 15:18-19)

29. If sickness is the will of God, then would not every physician be a law-breaker, every trained nurse be defying the Almighty, every hospital a house of rebellion instead of a house of mercy, and instead of supporting hospitals should we not then do our utmost to close them?

30. Since Jesus in the Gospels never commissioned anybody to preach the Gospel without commanding them to heal the sick, how can we obey this command if there is no Gospel (good news) of healing to proclaim to the sick as a basis for their faith? Or, since faith is expecting God to keep His promise, how can there be faith for healing if God has not promised it? And since the Bible is full of promises of healing are they not all Gospel (good news) to the sick? Since "faith cometh by hearing . . . the Word," how can the sick have faith for healing if there is nothing for them to hear?

31. Could the loving heart of the Son of God, Who had compassion upon the sick, and healed all who had need of healing, cease to regard the sufferings of His own when He had become exalted at the right hand of the Father?

ABOUT THE AUTHOR

Gregory Dixon is a media consultant and author who has written numerous Christian living and biographical books. Notable figures he has produced books for include Charlie "Tremendous" Jones (3 million copy bestselling author of *Life Is Tremendous*) and Ken Blanchard (18-million-copy best-selling author of 48 books). He has also been commissioned by leading publishers to work on projects for various best-selling authors such as Joyce Meyer, Reggie White, and others.

Gregory Dixon is also the author of the biographical account about the Temple University founder entitled *Acres of Diamonds: The Russell Conwell Story* and has written several other books. In addition, he conducts seminars related to the various topics he has written about in his various articles and books.

Passionate about spreading biblical values, Gregory Dixon has also answered the call to the ministry and he presently resides in Jacksonville, Florida.

45855041R00095

Made in the USA
Middletown, DE
15 July 2017